W9-BPK-891

30-MINUTE
RESUME
MAKEOVER

rev up your resume in half an hour

LOUISE KURSMARK

jist *Works*
America's Career Publisher®

LaRock

30-MINUTE RESUME MAKEOVER

© 2008 by Louise Kursmark

Published by JIST Works, an imprint of JIST Publishing
7321 Shadeland Station, Suite 200
Indianapolis, IN 46256-3923
Phone: 800-648-JIST   Fax: 877-454-7839   E-mail: info@jist.com

Visit our Web site at **www.jist.com** for information on JIST, free job search tips, tables of contents and sample pages, and ordering instructions for our many products!

Quantity discounts are available for JIST books. Have future editions of JIST books automatically delivered to you on publication through our convenient standing order program. Please call our Sales Department at 800-648-5478 for a free catalog and more information.

Trade Product Manager: Lori Cates Hand
Development Editor: Mike Thomas
Interior Designer: Aleata Halbig
Page Layout: Toi Davis
Cover Designers: Alan Evans and Katy Bodenmiller
Proofreaders: Linda Seifert, Jeanne Clark
Indexer: Joy Dean Lee

Printed in the United States of America
13 12 11 10 09 08   9 8 7 6 5 4 3 2 1

    Library of Congress Cataloging-in-Publication Data

Kursmark, Louise.
    30-minute resume makeover : rev up your resume in half an hour / Louise Kursmark.
        p. cm.
    Includes index.
    ISBN 978-1-59357-570-0 (alk. paper)
    1. Résumés (Employment) I. Title.
    HF5383.K865 2008
    650.14'2--dc22
                                    2008021158

ISBN 978-1-59357-570-0

About This Book

You want or need to get your job search in high gear. What's holding you back? If you're like most people, you don't have an updated resume. Or you have a resume that lacks the power and pizzazz you need to compete in a crowded job market against hundreds (if not thousands) of candidates who can easily find out about the same jobs you're applying for.

In short, you're not prepared or not competitive. And you need to fix that—fast.

30-Minute Resume Makeover is the resource you need for a fast transformation of your existing resume. Chapter 1 leads off with a Resume Report Card to help you assess whether your current resume answers employers' burning questions and positions you at the top of the candidate pool. To help you boost your grades to "A" in every category, I relate each employer question to specific 30-Minute Resume Makeover Strategies.

Chapter 2 leads you through the practical, logical, and easy-to-implement Makeover Strategies so you can build a winning resume from first word to last. Whether you need to ramp up your accomplishments, emphasize relevant keywords, or overcome employer red flags, chapter 2 shows you and tells you what to do and how to do it.

With your completed resume draft, you're ready for chapter 3, which describes a step-by-step review process for polishing your rough draft into a shining document. You'll also learn the correct process for creating a text version of your resume for online applications.

Next, browse through the before-and-after examples in chapter 4 to see how professional resume writers addressed real challenges that may be similar to your own circumstances. By rewriting, repositioning, reemphasizing, and reformatting, they transformed ho-hum resumes into standout documents showcasing very competitive candidates.

Chapter 5 addresses a critical companion to the resume—the cover letter. You'll learn strategies and success tips for making your cover letters as powerful as your resume. A gallery of cover letters gives you professional examples to use as your starting point.

Finally, in chapter 6, move on from *writing* your resume to *using* your resume, as you learn about the most efficient and effective means for you to find your next job.

In a condensed package, this book provides comprehensive A-to-Z advice for quickly improving your resume and launching your job search. The strategies help you create a resume that will do more than summarize your career history—it will sell, tell, and yell your capabilities to your next employer.

—Louise Kursmark

Acknowledgments

While writing this book, I was immersed in the inaugural class of a new training program I co-founded called Resume Writing Academy. I am especially grateful to my RWA students for giving me the opportunity to deconstruct and explain all of the strategies I've amassed during more than 20 years as a professional resume writer! It helped immensely in laying out the principles in this book, and the students generously shared their before-and-after resume transformations that appear in chapter 4.

My partner in the Resume Writing Academy, numerous books, and other ventures, Wendy Enelow, is an important part of my life and I value her wisdom, generosity, and *extreme* action orientation! Without her "do it now" mentality, many of our great ideas would still be on the drawing board. And last but far from least, I thank my husband, Bob Kursmark, for his forbearance as deadlines approach and his constant encouragement to reach for the next star.

Contents

Chapter 3: Proofread and Polish to Perfection 51

Chapter 4: Before-and-After Resume Transformations ..59

Chapter 1

Resume Diagnosis

C onsider the vast changes that have taken place in the world of work in
the last decade or so:

- The rise of a global economy, where job seekers as well as companies
  must compete beyond their local markets

- The emergence of the Internet as an immediate, always-available
  source for job information

- The birth of Web 2.0 interactive career sites offering customized
  applications and immediate feedback to Web-surfing candidates

- The growth of a mobile workforce, happy to jump to a new assignment, new job, or new company as opportunities ebb and flow

Yet in this constantly shifting environment, that sturdy old standby, the
resume, remains a primary tool for securing a new job.

But that doesn't mean you can produce a bland, traditional, "same-old"
resume and expect to get results. Given the fast pace of today's information
economy and the ease of applying to multiple jobs simultaneously, your
resume must do more than simply list your work history, job duties, and
educational credentials. To distinguish you from the crowed, your resume
must make your strongest "selling points" instantly evident to employers
and recruiters—not to mention automated resume scanners.

In a typical application scenario, you are competing against hundreds, if
not thousands, of other job seekers. All of the resumes are first reviewed by
keyword-matching scanners looking for the perfect fit. Then, if your
resume makes it past stage one, it might be glanced at by busy staff who
need to winnow down a large stack to a manageable pile. Finally, if it
makes its way to the hiring manager, it will vie with the resumes of other
highly qualified people who are just as intent as you are on landing the perfect job.

In short, it's a tough world out there and your resume must be up to the
task.

How Does Your Resume Stack Up?

This book is designed to *tell* you and *show* you exactly what you need to do to transform your resume from ho-hum to powerful, effective, and unique.

Because the first step in troubleshooting is pinpointing precisely what the problem is, in this chapter I will diagnose the most common resume problems and give you an easy-to-use Resume Report Card that will help you to identify and prioritize your resume challenges. In chapter 2, you'll begin your 30-Minute Resume Makeover by tackling each issue in priority order so you will make quick, logical progress in ramping up your resume to today's standards.

> **Tip:** *Even if your resume is rough, incomplete, or outdated, it's a jumping-off point for the 30-Minute Resume Makeover. If you don't have even a draft resume, use the worksheet in the appendix to organize and capture your essential information. Then return to this chapter to diagnose your initial effort and begin your Makeover.*

Look at It from the Employer's Perspective

Let's start by shifting perspective. When constructing a resume, most people begin by thinking, "What have I done? What do I want to do? What do I do best?" While all of these questions are important in helping you define your career goals, never forget that you must write your resume to appeal to your prime audience—employers and recruiters. With this in mind, it's helpful to begin the process by looking at your resume from the employer's point of view.

The following nine questions are written from the perspective of your potential employers. These are the questions they are asking as they scan, review, and more closely read your resume in search of their next great hire.

As you read the discussion surrounding each point, examine your resume to see if it measures up and use the Resume Report Card to grade yourself. Then, using the 30-Minute Makeover Strategies provided for each point, you can begin the quick, step-by-step process of building a "grade A" resume.

Employer Question #1: "Who are you?"

Employers seek an immediate answer to this question. They want to know, within split seconds of glancing at your resume, just "who" you are—what job functions you perform, what level you have achieved in your career, and what areas of the company they can sort you into. If they can't figure this out, they might glance down to your past job titles and make an assumption, or they might toss you into the "maybe" pile for review later—which usually means never, given the vast number of resumes they must wade through in a typical hiring cycle.

Your job, then, is to be hit-them-over-the-head obvious about who you are, beginning with the summary at the very top of your resume.

Before: Vague, non-specific, and non-memorable

> Experienced professional with a track record of contributing to organizational success. Excellent oral and written communication skills. Strong computer proficiency and ability to quickly learn and adapt to new responsibilities.

After: Clear, specific, and sharply focused

> Experienced **SALES MANAGER** with a 10-year track record of double-digit revenue and profit gains in highly competitive technology and telecommunications industries. Motivational leader who inspires sales teams to consistently outperform goals. Top performer in introducing new products in new markets—built both TeleTalk and Wellspring to #1 market share.

To assess whether your resume is instantly communicating "who you are," test-drive it with several friends or colleagues. Hand them your resume, wait five seconds, and snatch it back. Then ask them, "OK, who am I? What do you know about me from my resume?" If they can't answer quickly and clearly, you haven't answered the employer's question overtly enough.

30-Minute Makeover Strategies to Answer the Question, "Who are you?"

- Start with a Superlative Summary (page 27)
- Emphasize Experience and Accomplishments (page 37)

RESUME REPORT CARD

Grade your resume using the traditional A through F scale employed by classroom teachers.

A = Outstanding

B = Good

C = Average

D = Below Average

F = Failing

1. Who are you? _____

Grade _____

Does your resume instantly communicate essential identifying information that helps employers categorize you and creates context for the rest of the resume?

2. What can you do for me? _____

Grade _____

Does your resume include specific, measurable achievements that are relevant to your current job goals and demonstrate value to your next employer?

3. Do you have the skills I'm looking for? _____

Grade _____

Are your core skills easily identifiable, and do they match the keywords from the job description or posting?

4. Where have you worked before? _____

Grade _____

Can an employer quickly determine your job history—where you've worked, what job titles you've held, and how long you've worked at each company and each job?

5. Is your experience relevant to my needs? _____

Grade _____

Have you provided concise job descriptions that let your potential employer know the scope of your responsibilities—without providing so much detail that they lose interest?

6. Do you have the right education and credentials? _____

Grade _____

Are your education and credentials presented in a succinct and easy-to-spot format? Have you used the proper terminology and the appropriate level of detail?

7. What kind of person are you? _____

Grade _____

Does your resume include any "extra" information that can help a potential employer decide if you are a good fit for their job and company?

8. Do I see any "red flags" in your background? _____

Grade _____

Does your resume call attention to areas of concern, such as employment gaps or career instability? If so, is there enough other positive information so an employer is inclined at least to give you a call?

9. Can I easily get in touch with you? _____

Grade _____

Are your valid phone number and e-mail address prominently featured on your resume?

Employer Question #2: "What can you do for me?"

Employers care about much more than your job titles, education, and credentials. Your resume must show that you will be an asset to the company, someone who adds more value than cost.

The best way to demonstrate your *future* value to an employer is to show your *past* value. If you've been a consistent contributor to the success of an organization, employers can assume that you will continue to contribute. Thus, you want to describe experiences in which you have added value. Many of these experiences will come from your past work history, but you can pull them from other areas of your life as well, such as classroom projects, volunteer activities, and non–work-related roles.

To be truly compelling, these examples must be *specific* and *measurable* accomplishments that demonstrate your capabilities and your value. Be sure to cite numbers and other details. Most people do not—in fact, this is one of the most common failings in the thousands of resumes I review every year. Be explicit about your accomplishments and you will position yourself head and shoulders above other candidates!

Before: Vague, non-specific, meaningless accomplishments

> Introduced new accounting software that cut costs and speeded the month-end closing process.
>
> Participated on restructuring team to increase efficiency across the entire organization.

After: Precise, credible, meaningful accomplishments

> Cut costs by $800K annually and speeded month-end closing from 8 days to 8 hours by introducing new accounting software.
>
> Selected as department representative to restructuring team that implemented 37 enterprise-wide initiatives, adding $17M to the bottom line through waste reduction and efficiency improvement.

Now, assess your resume with a critical eye for the all-important accomplishments. Because this is truly the most important component of your resume, be a tough grader. Are all or most of your accomplishments quantified? Do the accomplishments and results jump off the page? Do you show a clear trend of adding value in every position of your career? Unless you can answer yes to every question, your resume needs remedial work.

30-Minute Makeover Strategies to Answer the Question, "What can you do for me?"

- Start with a Superlative Summary (page 27)
- Emphasize Experience and Accomplishments (page 37)

Employer Question #3: "Do you have the skills I'm looking for?"

Every job requires a set of fundamental skills. Employers include these skills in their postings and job descriptions, for the obvious reason that they want to hire someone who can perform the basic functions of the job. Therefore, to be considered as a viable candidate, your resume must include the right words and show that you have relevant experience using the core skills.

Before: Non-specific skills summary

> Strong programming skills and experience with a wide array of operating systems, development environments, and tools.

After: Keyword-rich skills summary

> - **Programming Languages/Standards:** HTML, CSS, JavaScript, XML, XHTML, ASP, JSP, Java, Perl, C, Ruby on Rails
>
> - **Operating Systems:** UNIX, IRIX, LINUX, Win 98/NT, DOS, Mac OS
>
> - **Development Environments and Methodologies:** ClearCase, Visual Basic Studio, Extreme Programming, EMACS, VI, UNIX
>
> - **Databases, CRM Tools, and Protocols:** Access, Oracle, ODBC, Vantive, SQL

As you review your resume, check to see whether it includes all or almost all of the keywords for your target jobs. If not, you won't make it past the initial computerized scan.

30-Minute Makeover Strategies to Answer the Question, "Do you have the skills I'm looking for?"

- Start with a Superlative Summary (page 27)

- Emphasize Experience and Accomplishments (page 37)

Employer Question #4: "Where have you worked before?"

As I've mentioned, hiring authorities are busy people. They need to quickly ascertain whether your qualifications match their needs. One of the things they'll consider is your employment track record—where have you worked, for how long, and with what job titles?

Regardless of whether you choose a chronological or functional format for your resume (see chapter 2), readers should be able to find and review your work history quickly and easily. What's more, they should be able to glean some information about your past employers—the size of each company, what it does, where it's located, and perhaps the markets in which it competes.

Before: Confusing and possibly misleading job history

EMPLOYMENT HISTORY, 2003–Present

Sales Representative at ABC Company and XYZ Office Products
Telephone Sales for XYZ Office Products
Macy's, part-time Retail Clerk and Seasonal Assistant

After: Clear, easy-to-understand career chronology

ABC COMPANY, 2007–Present
($100M reseller of distressed merchandise to bulk and odd-lot retailers)
Sales Representative

XYZ OFFICE PRODUCTS, 2003–2007
(Largest privately held office products company in the Midwest)
Outside Sales Representative, 2005–2007
Telephone Sales Representative, 2003–2005

MACY'S, 2000–2003 (part-time)
(Nation's #1 department store chain; $27B annual sales)
Retail Clerk—Men's Shoes, 2001–2003
Seasonal Assistant—Menswear, 2000 Holiday Season

A quick check of your resume should reveal whether you've answered this employer question or if you need to clarify the details and improve the presentation of your employment history.

30-Minute Makeover Strategy to Answer the Question, "Where have you worked before?"

- Emphasize Experience and Accomplishments (page 37)

Employer Question #5: "Is your experience relevant to my needs?"

Employers need to know whether you have experience performing functions similar to those that will be required for the job they're filling. Sometimes this information can be evident from your job titles—if you've worked as an Accounting Supervisor, and the opening is for an Accounting Supervisor or Accounting Manager, readers will assume you have relevant experience. But it's not always this clear-cut.

For example, one "inside sales representative" might perform pure sales functions—prospecting, cold-calling, pre-determining needs, and setting appointments for the sales team. Another person with the same title might function primarily as a customer service representative, responding to calls from existing customers, tracking down orders, resolving quality issues, and straightening out billing complaints. If the employer is looking for an aggressive "hunter" salesperson, this second candidate might not have the necessary experience for the job. Thus, it's important to clarify the scope and function of each job so employers can determine if your experience is relevant.

Don't, however, provide descriptions that are so lengthy and detailed that they "deaden" your resume. Keep these sections crisp, lively, and relevant—giving employers just the information they need to evaluate your candidacy.

Before: Insufficient job description

> **Senior Accountant,** performing full range of accounting responsibilities.

Before: Overly detailed job description

> Senior Accountant
>
> - Manage full cycle of accounts payable: Effectively communicate with headquarters to recommend effective accounting measures to resolve price discrepancies. Issue checks and make wire transfer payments. Carry out reimbursement of employees' expense reports.

(continued)

(continued)

- Perform accrual revenues and accounts receivable: Carry out timely AR collections, manage internal accounts and daily cash flow, and perform monthly cash projections. Analyze and communicate with buyers for discrepancies, resolve payment, and issue debit/credit memos for RMA returns. Perform accounts reconciliation in support of month-end and year-end closing.

- Maintain monthly inventory reports and physical inventory counting: Consolidate inventory reports from consignment locations and perform monthly inventory reconciliation. Analyze inventory movements and effectively monitor consignment stock and ensure accurate inventory valuation.

After: Concise, readable, and highly relevant description of on-the-job experience

Senior Accountant: Performed a full range of accounting responsibilities, including A/P, A/R, collections, and inventory reporting and reconciliation. Reconciled all G/L accounts to support month-end and year-end closings.

As you'll learn in chapter 2, overly detailed job descriptions are a common flaw in many resumes. Your goal is to be relevant, interesting, and as brief as possible in communicating the essential information. How do you grade yourself in this area?

30-Minute Makeover Strategies to Answer the Question, "Is your experience relevant to my needs?"

- Emphasize Experience and Accomplishments (page 37)
- Enhance with Education and "Extras" (page 44)
- Proofread and Polish to Perfection (page 49)

Employer Question #6: "Do you have the right education and credentials?"

Among the requirements for many jobs are educational credentials such as a bachelor's degree or a specific technical certification. If you have the qualification, be sure it is featured prominently in your resume! If employers or resume scanners overlook or misinterpret the information, you will be passed over.

On the other hand, if you lack a specific educational qualification, you might not be given a chance at a job for which you are otherwise qualified—and you might be tempted to "fudge the facts" a bit to get your foot in the door. But misleading employers about your qualifications is a bad strategy that is likely to backfire. Instead, present your education as advantageously as possible to give yourself a fighting chance. And even more importantly, review the discussion in chapter 6 about the job search strategies that are most effective for everyone, regardless of your qualifications.

Finally, remember to use commonly accepted terminology to present your education. Keywords count in this section of your resume, too.

Before: Unclear educational credential and unnecessary detail about college activities

> • Degree in business from Hudson, 1989. Cum laude, 3.5 GPA. Courses in economics, accounting, marketing, general management, human resources, business plan preparation, and effective presentations. Member of senior class events committee and intramural volleyball.

After: Crisp, correct, and succinct presentation of educational qualifications

> • Bachelor of Science in Business Administration, cum laude—Hudson University

Review the education section of your resume and grade yourself on how cleanly and clearly you have presented the key information and how positively you have presented it.

30-Minute Makeover Strategies to Answer the Question, "Do you have the right education and credentials?"

• Enhance with Education and "Extras" (page 44)

Employer Question #7: "What kind of person are you?"

When scanning resumes, employers first look for a skills and experience fit. Once those fundamentals are covered, they search for more insightful information to distinguish you from other qualified candidates. Because all candidates will possess the basic job requirements, it is often the intangibles that determine who is invited to interview and who is ultimately hired.

Together, these "soft" skills and character attributes make up what is known as your "personal brand." Good definitions of a personal brand are "your unique promise of value" and "a collection of perceptions in the mind of the consumer." In other words, your brand describes what people feel, sense, and know about you. It communicates not just what you do, but how you do it and the value that creates. If you can communicate your personal brand in your resume, you will clearly distinguish yourself from others with similar skills sets. You'll be more memorable, and you'll establish—in advance of any interview—what it is that makes you different and special.

Adding insightful information about what makes you special can be a definite plus on your resume and can help decision-makers discriminate between you and another candidate, even before you've met in person.

Branding statements and "extra" information can be woven into your summary and mentioned in your accomplishments. In addition, you can consolidate many different "extras" into separate sections at the end of the resume, as shown in the following examples.

Before: Overly detailed "extra" information

FOREIGN LANGUAGES:
Proficient in Arabic and French languages with superb familiarity with culture, religion, and habits of most Asian, Middle Eastern, and European countries.

COMPUTER PROFICIENCIES:
Proficient and possess the necessary skills in working with computers and information technology tools including but not limited to Microsoft office bundles such as Word, Excel, Access, and PowerPoint; most PCs; and Windows XP, Me, Vista, NT, and others.

Ability to work with ACT; Adobe Illustrator, Photoshop, PageMaker, and Flash; and Subscriber Management System (CSG).

HOBBIES:
Skiing, racquetball, and swimming

TRAVEL:
Japan, UAE, France, England, Lebanon, Jordan, Egypt, Kuwait, Saudi Arabia, Italy, Netherlands, Singapore, Philippines, Thailand, Israel, Bahrain, Qatar, Germany, India, Mexico, Canada, Serbia, Kosovo, Macedonia, Albania, and many more

After: Effective presentation of "extras" that are relevant to this candidate's goal of an international management position and reveal leadership skills, community spirit, and ability to secure support for ideas

Global Languages and Culture: Proficient in Arabic and French. Widely traveled and conversant with business cultures in Asia, Middle East, and Europe.

Professional Memberships:

- American Marketing Association—DC chapter

- Arab-American Marketing Association

Activities: Competitive swimmer and racquetball player. Organized swimming league for inner-city youth and led for 7 years. Raised $10K–$15K yearly to support pool maintenance and participation at regional meets.

Evaluate your resume to see if your personality shines through. If your resume reads like a generic job description or contains only the trite attributes that can be found on every other resume ("strong interpersonal communication skills"), you have lots of room for improvement.

30-Minute Makeover Strategies to Answer the Question, "What kind of person are you?"

- Start with a Superlative Summary (page 27)

- Enhance with Education and "Extras" (page 44)

Employer Question #8: "Do I see any 'red flags' in your background?"

For long-term success, companies need to build a strong, solid pool of employees while keeping their hiring costs under control. Thus, good companies hire not just for their needs today, but for their goals tomorrow. They want to avoid "bad hires" and high turnover. So they'll be looking at your resume for any information that signals you are not a steady or productive employee.

Any of the following might be considered a "red flag" to employers:

- Long gaps between employment
- Many short-term jobs ("job hopping")
- An erratic career track—veering from one field to another without apparent purpose
- Lack of evidence that you performed well on the job
- Demotion
- Too much time in the same job
- Misspellings, poor grammar, poor writing, or obvious errors
- Resumes that are too long (3+ pages)
- Resumes that lack substance
- Functional resumes that don't make it clear where and when you acquired your skills and experience

By following the advice in this book, you'll quickly eliminate many of these issues. You'll have a concise, powerful, accomplishment-focused resume that highlights your relevant skills.

But not everyone has a textbook career. If any of the red flags are of concern to you, pay careful attention to the discussion in chapter 2 about your specific challenges, and follow the recommendations to de-emphasize them on your resume.

And be sure to read chapter 6 in-depth to learn how to conduct an effective job search through networking rather than relying on automated resume-scanning or high-volume searches that can easily place your resume in the rejection pile. In fact, no matter what your circumstances, be sure to read chapter 6! Even in today's electronic age, the majority of people find jobs through personal contacts, not through an online ad or a resume posting site. Chapter 6 is your guide to finding a job as quickly and efficiently as possible.

30-Minute Makeover Strategies to Answer the Question, "Do I see any 'red flags' in your background?"

- Fashion a Strong Framework (page 20)
- Start with a Superlative Summary (page 27)
- Emphasize Experience and Accomplishments (page 37)
- Proofread and Polish to Perfection (page 49)

Employer Question #9: "Can I easily get in touch with you?"

It seems obvious, but you might be surprised at the number of people who forget to include their phone number, e-mail address, or even their name on their resume! Or they format this important data in a tiny font size or in gray ink as a discreet footnote. A pet peeve of some hiring authorities is too much contact information—two or three phone numbers, more than one e-mail address, fax number, pager, and so forth. They don't know which method to use—or worse, they have to make three or four attempts before they can reach you.

You can avoid irritating and frustrating employers simply by formatting your name and contact information so that it's easy to find and easy to read—and by quickly responding to phone calls and e-mail messages.

Before: Small, hard-to-read contact information

781-555-2495

jwilliams@yahoo.com

249 North Main Street, Malden, MA 02148

James Williams

After: Easy-to-find, easy-to-read, attractively formatted contact information

---

James Williams

781-555-2495
jwilliams@yahoo.com
249 North Main Street, Malden, MA 02148

A quick check of your resume should reveal whether you've made it easy or challenging for employers to contact you. Grade yourself accordingly.

30-Minute Makeover Strategies to Answer the Question, "Can I easily get in touch with you?"

- Fashion a Strong Framework (page 20)
- Proofread and Polish to Perfection (page 49)

Did You Get All A's?

Now that you've graded your resume in nine distinct areas, review your Resume Report Card to see how it measures up. If you earned all A's, congratulations! You are ready to launch your job search—you can move quickly to chapter 5, "Create a Killer Cover Letter," and chapter 6, "Find a Job Fast," and start putting your resume to work.

Of course, most resumes will need a little tweaking and polishing, and a few will require a major rewrite. Pinpoint the appropriate 30-Minute Makeover Strategies that address your specific needs, then use chapter 2 to implement those strategies and boost your B, C, D, and F grades to A level.

Key Points: Chapter 1

- In today's competitive job market and with the ease of electronic communication, your resume must stand out and be compelling to vie with dozens or hundreds of other candidates for your target positions.

- Your resume must quickly answer the nine questions that employers ask themselves as they review resumes to select candidates to interview:

  - Who are you?

  - What can you do for me?

  - Do you have the skills I'm looking for?

  - Where have you worked before?

  - Is your experience relevant to my needs?

  - Do you have the right education and credentials?

  - What kind of person are you?

  - Do I see any "red flags" in your background?

  - Can I easily get in touch with you?

- Grade yourself on these nine questions using the Resume Report Card and then begin your 30-Minute Resume Makeover in chapter 2.

Chapter 2

Resume Repair: The 30-Minute Resume Makeover

Now that you know where your resume needs to be strengthened, this chapter *tells* you and *shows* you how to do it through detailed explanations of each of the 30-Minute Makeover Strategies.

To achieve a noticeable improvement in your resume for each 30 minutes you spend, look at your Resume Report Card in chapter 1 and identify where you need the most improvement. A good tactic is to give top priority to those areas where you scored the lowest and move on to your mid-level and higher grades as you have time.

Another approach would be to quickly spiff up the sections where you earned B grades, then plunge in-depth into the areas where your resume needs more serious help.

If your time is extremely limited and you have to choose just one area to tackle, I recommend that you focus on Strategy #3: Emphasize Experience and Accomplishments. Your accomplishments are the jewels of your resume. They are most valued by employers and they are distinctly yours. Make them shine to gain the biggest payback from your Resume Makeover.

This chapter addresses each of the 30-Minute Makeover Strategies in logical order for making over your resume from the top down. Each section includes a discussion of the strategy, tips for applying the strategy to your resume, and examples of the strategy in action.

Keep in mind, there is not a single "recipe" for creating a great resume, and not every recommendation will be right for your specific circumstances. You'll need to evaluate the options, match up the strategy to your situation and the facts of your career, and make the choices that will allow you to best present your capabilities and value to a potential employer. The guidelines and examples will help, and the before-and-after samples in chapter 4 will show you how professional resume writers have addressed a variety of resume-writing challenges.

In the end, your resume will be unique—just as you are—and showcase the distinctive experience, credentials, accomplishments, and potential you bring to your next employer.

STRATEGY #1: Fashion a Strong Framework

Before you begin writing, think about how to structure your resume in a way that makes it easy to read and quickly communicates your key value. Two factors that come into play are

- Organization—in what order do you place your information?

- Design—how do you present the information on the page?

No matter what you've been told, or how you've structured your resume in the past, take a fresh look at these options to be sure you're making smart choices for your current circumstances.

Organizational Format: Chronological or Functional?

For most job seekers, the most advantageous format for your resume is a **reverse chronological/hybrid format** that includes the following elements:

- **A summary or profile** that paints a crisp word picture of "who you are" and highlights your key skills and most impressive career achievements.

- **Your reverse-chronological career history,** beginning with your most recent position and proceeding back in time to the beginning of your career. This chronological section includes both **position descriptions** and **career achievements.**

- **Education and "extras"**—the credentials, activities, and additional experiences that round out your qualifications.

The reverse-chronological format is vastly preferred by recruiters and employers because it gives them a solid framework for evaluating your career. They can easily find the information they seek regarding your career history, the length of time you have held each job, your education, and other credentials. They don't have to hunt to find the facts they need.

The reverse-chronological format is beneficial to you, too, because it allows you to show how you've progressed in your career and to highlight your important achievements in each role. By leading off with a powerful summary, you can position yourself appropriately and call attention to your most impressive qualifications right up front.

Follow these guidelines to maximize the effectiveness of your reverse-chronological resume.

Reverse-Chronological Resume Tips

- Be certain that your Summary/Profile is carefully targeted for your current career goals rather than simply providing an overview of your entire career.

- Within your chronological work history, show your total tenure with each company as well as time in each job.

- Clearly distinguish your job titles to illustrate your career progression.

- Keep your job descriptions crisp and relevant; otherwise, you will lose your readers' interest.

- Include specific, measurable achievements for every position.

- As you go further back in time, reduce the amount of space you allot for each position. Consider summarizing your earliest career history to keep the resume crisp and to avoid drawing attention to your age, especially if you are over 50. It's also fine to omit some jobs and simply focus on the most recent and most relevant.

RANDY LOWE

617-823-4949   249 Marlborough Street, Boston, MA 02116   rlowe@gmail.com

MARKETING
PRODUCT MANAGEMENT ▶ PRODUCT DEVELOPMENT ▶ PACKAGING

Track record of revenue growth, profit enhancement, and successful product-line management during 9 years in progressively challenging marketing roles. Strong foundation in market research and technology paired with creativity and the ability to innovate. Talent for leading and inspiring teams to top performance.

- **Set new business directions** by recognizing and seizing market opportunities.
- **Improved performance in all products and brands managed;** grew revenues, cut costs, developed unique retailer programs and packages, and improved brand image.
- **Effectively prioritized multiple projects** to align results with business objectives.

EXPERIENCE

CORE CORPORATION, INC., Woburn, MA   1998–2008
($180M public company manufacturing and marketing consumer comfort products. Marquee brand is HappyFeet; key accounts include Wal-Mart, Macy's, and other national retailers.)

SENIOR MARKETING MANAGER, 2005–2008—Led marketing strategy and programs for 3 product lines totaling $150M sales. Coordinated the efforts of design, product development, and manufacturing to deliver products for seasonal deadlines. Directed development of marketing communications; planned and led national sales meetings; developed and delivered seasonal product updates to the sales force. Managed $4M budget.

Increased sales and profitability in all 3 brand segments:

- **Value Brands:**
  —Boosted profit margins from **25%** to **39%** through continuous improvement efforts that removed cost from every point of production—sourcing, production, packaging, distribution.
  —Grew Wal-Mart program from **$3M** to **$7M** by identifying and capitalizing on sales trends.

- **HappyFeet™:**
  —Created and launched Premier Collection, increasing total brand sales **60%** (**$5.8M** to **$9.3M**).
  —Redesigned product displays to accommodate **20%** more product without increasing costs.

- **CoreComfort™:**
  —Worked with manufacturing on technology-based line restage; product sales increased **31%**.
  —Developed new packaging that increased inventory flexibility and saved **$95K** in first year.

PRODUCT MANAGER, 2001–2005—Recruited to join newly strengthened marketing team and challenged to improve performance of both private-label and branded products.

- Contributed to record sales performance, 2001: **$148M, 9%** growth over prior year.
- Developed POP sales program that increased retail space by more than **200%**.
- Spearheaded a packaging restage that generated **$8.1M** in incremental sales, reduced packaging costs **15%**, and improved packaging image and brand identification.

MARKETING ASSISTANT, 1998–2001

EDUCATION

MBA—Concentration: Marketing Management   Babson College, Wellesley, MA, 2005
BSBA—Concentration: Management   Boston College, Chestnut Hill, MA, 1999

Figure 2.1: A reverse-chronological resume.

For some job seekers, however, a chronological format won't work well. If you've been out of the workforce for a while, if you are changing careers, or if your past experience pigeonholes you in an industry that you don't want to pursue, you might want to use a **functional** resume, which typically follows this structure:

- **A summary or profile** that paints a crisp word picture of "who you are." Your summary might be preceded by an **objective statement** that clearly establishes your current job targets.

- **A presentation of your key skills** accompanied by **achievements** that demonstrate your skills; these skills and achievements can be drawn from any and all of your experiences, from your earliest jobs, classroom experiences, and outside activities as well as your more recent professional history. This "functional" section of your resume typically occupies the most space.

- **A brief listing of your work experience**, usually including just job titles, employer names, and dates, but without the position descriptions and accomplishments that are typical of the chronological resume.

The advantage to a functional resume is that it allows you to pull together diverse experiences into a cohesive whole by grouping these experiences according to functional expertise. For example, if you are a new graduate, you can create a functional section called "Leadership Experience" and include leadership activities in the classroom, in your part-time jobs, and in your volunteer activities. Together, these paint a picture of someone who has proven leadership skills even if you don't have tons of relevant experience on the job.

Similarly, if you are changing careers or returning to work after an extended absence, a functional format will allow you to paint the right picture up front without calling attention to your unrelated work experience or lack of recent employment.

Be aware, however, that employers tend to dislike functional resumes because they can't always tell when and where you used your skills or earned your experience. They don't know if an accomplishment is recent or many years old, and they wonder if you are hiding something by not presenting a straightforward chronology.

By all means, use the functional format if it is the best way to present your skills and experience. The following tips will help you minimize employer "red flags."

Functional Resume Tips

- Carefully select functional headings that relate to the jobs you are targeting. This is a great way to include relevant keywords in your resume. Then, write specific and measurable achievement statements for each of those functional areas.

- Be sure to provide a chronological work history, usually as the last section of your functional resume, so readers can quickly find it and consider it as they review your accomplishments. However, it's perfectly all right to omit some of your jobs if they are irrelevant to your current goals.

- Consider including a brief mention of where and when each accomplishment occurred. You can place it in parentheses or italics at the end of the accomplishment statement. This can help reassure readers about the relevance of your experience.

- If possible, keep your resume to one page. This lets readers consider all the information in one view, without having to flip pages back and forth to compare your work history with your achievements.

- On a contrary note, if you prefer that readers *not* get an immediate look at your career history, create a strong and detailed functional achievement section on page 1 and perhaps spilling over to page 2. Hope that you'll so impress them with what you've accomplished, they won't focus on the fact that your experience is not recent or particularly relevant.

Cynthia Evans

317-249-7590 Home • 317-217-9076 Mobile • evans@indy.rr.com
2594 West Allen Road, Indianapolis, IN 46218

CUSTOMER SERVICE PROFESSIONAL

Value Offered
- Record of top performance in demanding, high-volume customer-service roles.
- Strengths in organization, time management, and the development of efficient processes.
- Expert project management including meticulous note-taking and persistent follow-through.
- Customer-service orientation and effective communications skills at all levels.
- Impeccable record of attendance, timeliness, and dependability.

SKILLS AND ACCOMPLISHMENTS

Sales and Customer Service
- Achieved customer-satisfaction scores in the high 90s every year with Midwest Health.
- Secured 10 new client groups in 3 years—#1 in the region in sales group sales.
- For R.L. Stevens, consistently met or exceeded goal of 24-hour project turnaround while client load doubled.

Organization and Project Management
- Maintained detailed records of call history and created a foolproof follow-up system that ensured a consistent, persistent approach and led to excellent sales and service results.
- Wrote sales letters and executed mass mailings to target accounts.
- Planned and coordinated meetings, events, and educational programs.
- Managed a high volume of incoming calls without diminishing service levels or productivity.

Presentation and Communication
- Represented Midwest Health at hospital-based health fairs.
- Delivered informational presentations to new accounts; thoroughly explained operational procedures to ensure compliance and minimize problems.

Special Assignments
- Personally handled special projects for the Regional Director, such as cold-calling clients for contract updates and executing mass-marketing mailings. Finished all projects on or ahead of schedule and with consistently high quality and accuracy.
- Following merger, initiated hundreds of phone calls to introduce new accounts to Midwest Health and educate on policies/procedures.

CAREER HISTORY

Midwest Health Partners, Indianapolis, IN   2003–2008
- Provider Relations Representative, 2005–2008
- Office Manager, 2003–2005

R.L. Stevens, Indianapolis, IN   1999–2003
- Administrative Assistant

EDUCATION

Indiana University
Completed 75% of requirements for Bachelor of Arts in Liberal Arts

Figure 2.2: A functional resume.

Design Considerations: Design for Clarity

How you design your resume—the fonts you choose, the way you lay out the information, how you decide to highlight various elements, and where you place each piece of information—can have an enormous effect on how quickly and easily your readers will glean essential information about you.

Your goal is to make the resume easy to skim while providing meaningful and substantive information. You want readers' attention to be drawn to the most impressive things about you on first glance, and you need to package a lot of detailed information in a neat, concise, attractive presentation. The following guidelines will help.

Design Tips

- Choose a typeface that is standard on most computers (Arial, Arial Narrow, Book Antiqua, Bookman, Garamond, Georgia, Tahoma, Times New Roman, or Verdana). This will ensure readers view your resume just as you've prepared it.

- Use a readable type size—10 or 11 point for most fonts. But be aware that 10 point is too small to read comfortably in some fonts (such as Times New Roman), while 11 point appears too large and almost elementary in other fonts (such as Verdana and Bookman).

- Be sure your name and contact information can be easily found and quickly read. For resume scanning purposes, your name should be on the first line of the page.

- Define the different sections of your resume with headings and subheadings that guide the reader in identifying key information. Emphasize these headings with bold type and a larger font size.

- Keep your paragraphs short—no more than three or four lines. If the text is too dense, readers will skip over it, so break longer paragraphs into two or condense the text by removing extraneous information.

- Limit your lists of bullet points to four or five. If you have more items to include, group like items under subheadings that will break up a long list and help your readers quickly skim through the resume.

- Format your resume on one or two pages. In rare instances a resume can be longer than two pages, but be absolutely certain the information is essential.

- As your design skills permit, consider using enhancements such as bold and italic type, borders, shading, columns, and tables to create a distinctive yet professional appearance.

30-Minute Resume Makeover

Use the preceding guidance to ensure that your resume is appropriately structured and designed such that it's easy for readers to grasp essential information about you. To summarize the key points from this section:

> **Tip:** *Thumb through chapter 4, paying particular attention to the "after" examples. In many cases, in addition to rewriting the content, the writer transformed a bland, typical resume format into a distinctive, attractive design that draws attention to the most significant information. Look to these samples for your design inspiration.*

- Use a reverse-chronological format if at all possible; it is most preferred by employers.

- Use a functional format if it is truly the best way to position and present yourself.

- Choose the right fonts and font enhancements to make it easy for readers to skim the resume and pick up key facts, such as your contact information, your employers and job titles, and your career chronology.

- Organize your material into brief paragraphs and concise bullet points to promote readability.

- Add design elements to enhance the presentation of your resume while drawing favorable attention to your most notable qualifications.

STRATEGY #2: Start with a Superlative Summary

The first section of your resume—immediately below your name and contact information—can be called the Summary, Profile, Introduction, Overview, Qualifications Brief, or other title. Or it might have no title at all and simply begin with a headline that states your professional expertise. Regardless of what you call it, this section is a critical positioning piece that lets you establish, clearly and up front, who you are and your most important qualifications.

The Summary can take many forms and include many components. Most typically, your Summary will include some or all of the following:

- A headline and subheadings that clearly and quickly establish key facts about you and your expertise.

- A branding statement that distinguishes you from others with similar qualifications.

- A brief paragraph or two summarizing your professional qualifications.

- Your core skills, presented in a quick-read list that includes the essential keywords for your profession and your expertise.

- Your most notable career achievements, either included as part of the summary paragraphs or in a separate bullet-point list.

You can see all five of these components in this sample summary:

Strategic Marketing Executive

Marketing strategist, innovator, and tactical leader of enterprise-wide initiatives that build brand value and result in sustainable, profitable growth.

Driver and champion of transformational programs—able to gain executive sponsorship, build internal support at all levels, and create cross-functional project teams that deliver exceptional results. Expert in aligning strategy with organizational vision/goals and interpreting the voice of the customer through enhanced customer insight and knowledge management.

Proven professional with a strong record of results in diverse industries—financial services, healthcare/insurance, professional services, and packaged goods—both business-to-business and consumer.

Areas of Expertise
- Strategic Planning
- Consulting
- Market Research
- Product Development
- Market Segmentation
- Branding
- Advertising
- Direct Marketing
- CRM
- Customer Satisfaction
- Project Management
- Strategic Alliances

Career Highlights

- **Smythe Associates:** Delivered a branding and communications redesign that established progressive image and positioned firm for accelerated expansion in strategic market segments.

- **Pioneer Health Services:** Transitioned business division from risk-avoidance to risk-management strategy, introducing new product portfolios that drove sales up 50% and market share 40% in just 2 years.

- **Fifth Third Bank, Procter & Gamble:** Improved sales, profitability, and market share through creative marketing and new product initiatives focused on strategic goals and the bottom line.

There are many ways to format your Summary, and many choices for the information you might include. In fact, your Summary can be the most creative part of your resume! A good way to get some ideas for your Summary is to flip through the sample resumes in this book and see the variety of ways professional resume writers have structured the opening sections of their resumes.

Include Keywords

When employers read your resume, you want them immediately to perceive that you have the right blend of skills and experience for they job they are filling. To get this reaction your resume must contain the same words employers use to search for candidates. Without these keywords, you won't make it past the automatic resume scanners, and you won't strike the right chord with human viewers, either.

Keyword Tips

Use the following guidelines to ensure that your resume contains the right keywords for your job targets.

- Include, as appropriate, all of the generally accepted terms for your profession. Many of these terms will occur naturally as you write about your experience and achievements. For example, if you are an accountant, you're likely to use the terms A/R (Accounts Receivable) and A/P (Accounts Payable) when you describe your job responsibilities.

- Review postings for your target jobs, highlight the terms that crop up over and over, and use these in your resume. For example, if you're in sales, it's likely that postings will call for people with experience "prospecting and closing new business." If you have this experience, be sure to mention it in your resume!

- Consider creating a separate keyword section in your Summary, as shown on the preceding page and in many of the sample resumes in this book. Resume reviewers can quickly skim such a concentrated list, and it's easy for you to tweak your list just a bit for a perfect match with each job you apply for. However, automated scanners will find keywords anywhere in your resume, so if a separate list doesn't work for you, that's fine.

- Use a combination of nouns, verbs, and adjectives as keywords, and strive to present the really top terms in a variety of ways—for example, you could use both "customer service" and "consistently exceeded customer satisfaction goals" in your resume.

Use Postings to Find Keywords

Job postings are a rich source of keywords, which are <u>underlined</u> in the following excerpts from a well-known posting site:

Budget Analyst

The Budget Analyst will assist in the preparation and processing of departmental <u>operating budgets</u> and <u>projections</u> requiring <u>advanced budget analysis techniques</u>. The successful candidate must have a commitment to excellence and <u>accuracy</u>; good <u>organizational and analytical skills</u>; a <u>Bachelor's degree</u> in a job-related discipline; and <u>three years of experience</u> in <u>budget analysis and preparation</u> or <u>accounting</u>.

Marketing Manager

Seeking a <u>high-energy</u>, <u>innovative</u> <u>B2B marketing professional</u> (<u>4–7 years of experience</u>) who is accustomed to working in a <u>fast-paced</u>, <u>entrepreneurial</u> business environment. The candidate will assist in the development, management, and execution of a <u>strategic marketing plan</u>. The Marketing Manager is responsible for the management and execution of all <u>marketing campaigns</u>, <u>corporate Web site</u>, <u>lead generation programs</u>, <u>e-mail marketing</u>, and <u>event planning, management, and logistics</u>.

A good candidate would possess combined <u>creative</u> and <u>strategic</u> business skills, strong <u>communication</u> skills, <u>analytical</u> and <u>budgeting</u> skills, an <u>undergraduate degree in marketing</u> or <u>communications</u>. Must be a <u>team player</u> with good <u>interpersonal skills</u>. Must be willing to travel for <u>trade shows</u> and other events.

Compile a list of keywords for your profession, your industry, and your current job targets. After you've completed your resume draft, cross-check the list to be sure you've included most if not all of the keywords.

If you decide to create a separate keyword list in your Summary, keep your list to no more than 12 to 16 items that can be comfortably presented in a three- or four-column format. It should be designed to be easily skimmed.

Following is an example of a keyword section for a training specialist:

Key Areas of Strength

Executive Presentation Skills	Process Streamlining	Talent Management/Production
Professional Development	PR/Media Management	Sales Presentation/Negotiation
Persuasive Speaking	Speech Coaching	Consultative Selling Skills

Of course, it's not a good idea to annoy potential employers. So don't try the trick of packing your resume with keywords that don't apply to your experience. It won't take readers long to figure out that you really don't know what you're talking about and don't have the qualifications they're looking for.

Communicate Your Personal Brand

Why do some people buy Heinz ketchup, while others prefer Hunt's? The products are similar and used for identical purposes, yet for some definable or indefinable reasons consumers prefer one brand over another.

You might not think of yourself as a condiment, but in a similar way your brand is what sets you apart from others who are vying for the same jobs. Your brand might represent tangible benefits—perhaps you've achieved double-digit revenue growth every year of your career—as well as the less tangible qualities that make you the person you are and the employee you will be. Your strength might be getting others to support innovative ideas. Or maybe you see possibilities that others don't. Maybe, as a teacher, you are known for gaining parental support that far exceeds what your peers can achieve.

The following examples show brief branding statements that were included as a "tagline" in the Summary section of each resume.

Desktop support / field IT technician:

Decreasing idle time and cementing customer loyalty by identifying and solving complex IT issues

31

Senior management executive:

"I deliver growth for companies—every time." Accurately forecasting industry trends and consumer interests that allow companies to exceed revenue projections, maximize ROI performance, achieve strong profitability, and realize significant market growth.

Marketing executive:

Translating consumer insights to actionable strategies for dynamic business growth

Of course, before you can create a "zinger" brand statement for your resume, you'll need to define your brand—your unique combination of strengths, experience, skill sets, and personal attributes that together spell your value to an employer. The process of defining your brand can be complex and intensive. Yet getting a handle on what makes you unique can help you gain clarity about your ideal job fit. It can help you sell your advantages during interviews. And it will give you "market distinctiveness" now and throughout your career.

Questions to Help You Define Your Personal Brand

Stimulate your thinking with the following questions:

- What makes me different from others in my workplace?
- How do I stand out from others in my profession?
- How do others describe me?
- What am I known for?
- What is my reputation?
- What am I best at?
- What "firsts" can I claim?
- What do people remember about me?
- How am I able to succeed where others don't?
- What do I think are my greatest strengths, and how do these relate to performance on the job?

As you think through the answers to these questions, you should be able to identify themes and trends—things that have always been true about you in every job you've held and activity you've been involved with. Maybe, like Ronald Reagan, you are the "great communicator." Or like Tiger Woods, you're a dominant player driven to continuously improve and always win. Or like Avis, you put forth extra effort. We all have distinctive traits and consistent behaviors. These are the keys to your personal brand.

Translate your findings to language that you can use in your resume, beginning with the Summary and carrying through the remainder of the document. Your brand must be an authentic representation of who you are—not just a tagline. Therefore, your resume should be filled with examples that support your brand claims.

For example, if you claim to "decrease idle time" by "identifying and solving IT issues," be sure that you include some examples of time you saved and problems you solved. If you say you "deliver growth for companies—every time," you won't have much credibility unless your resume includes repeated examples of delivering growth.

If the idea of defining your personal brand intrigues you, you might want to consider working with a career coach who is also a Certified Personal Brand Specialist. A leading organization for personal branding is Reach Communications, and you can find a list of certified coaches at www.reachcc.com.

Highlight Your "Wow" Achievements

To capture the attention of busy, resume-overloaded employers, your most impressive achievements need to be blatantly obvious and truly impressive. A good way to achieve this level of impact is to create a separate section in your Summary called "Career Highlights" or "Performance Milestones" or "Key Results," where you highlight the top three, four, or five accomplishments of your career.

You might be thinking, why stop at four or five? Why not put all of my accomplishments front and center? I don't recommend this strategy, for the following reasons:

- Without the context of your career chronology, readers can't fully understand or appreciate what you've done.

- If your list is too long, they glide over it quickly without really reading.

- If they don't know your career history, they tend to flip immediately to the career chronology section, overlooking the accomplishment list you worked so hard to create.

Instead, grab readers' attention by highlighting just a few truly notable achievements in the Summary, as illustrated in the next two examples.

Career Highlights

- Co-founded biotech services company Bio Science Safety and generated **$1M** in first-year revenue.

- Identified buyer and executed divestiture of Baker's **$200M** Immunotherapy Division to RX Corporation.

- Spurred **40%** increase in medical-research patent filings in 1 year for a medical research institution.

- Generated **25%** annual sales growth in Biodiagnostics' In Vitro Business Unit for 3 straight years.

- Drove development of 15 medical diagnostic tests that generated **$500M** in sales in first 3 years for Midwest Labs.

PERFORMANCE HIGHLIGHTS: Sales Growth, Profitability, and Account Penetration

- **134%** revenue growth over 5 years

- **40%** to **70%** market share for every product in portfolio

- **42%** gross-margin improvement in the most challenging market in recent history

- **#1** revenue-generating product for 135-year-old company

Tips for Selecting and Presenting Your "Wow" Achievements

With the following strategies, you will immediately boost your Summary above the ordinary and let employers know what is truly distinctive about you.

- Write brief, punchy statements for hard-hitting impact; save the details for further down in your career chronology section.

- Include numbers and other specific results.

- Choose achievements that are closely related to your current career goals. Otherwise, your resume will look unfocused.

- You can select achievements from throughout your career, but try to include at least one recent highlight.

- Feel free to include accomplishments from activities outside your career, if they are relevant, appropriate, and impressive. This is a particularly effective strategy for people changing careers or returning to work after a period of unemployment.

Consider an Objective

Once upon a time, all resumes began with an Objective statement. In the past few decades, however, Objectives have been replaced by Summaries that provide a strong lead-in to today's hybrid/reverse-chronological resume.

In most situations a Summary is the most advantageous way to start your resume—it allows you to present the most relevant and beneficial information in capsule format to attract the attention of employers. But in a few instances, you might be better off beginning your resume with an Objective.

Consider the following scenarios:

- You are making a radical career change, and your past work history is totally unrelated to your current goals. In addition to choosing a functional format, you might want to start with an Objective that clearly communicates the type of jobs you are interested in.

- You are a new graduate without relevant work experience. An Objective makes it easy for employers to know what you're looking for.

- You have limited work experience, and what you have is "all over the map." Now, you've settled on a career direction, and an Objective might be the best way to communicate this information to employers.

- You want to customize your resume for each application without having to change anything except the Objective.

If you choose to use an Objective, don't fall into the trap of the trite, all-purpose openings that can be found on all too many resumes: "Seeking a challenging position with the opportunity to advance based on

performance." Objectives like these don't tell employers "who you are," and they take up valuable space on your resume with information that is essentially meaningless.

Use your Objective to communicate your goal as clearly and specifically as possible. In fact, you might want to mention the specific job and company for which you customized your resume. Then, enhance the Objective by mentioning some of the skills and value you offer, as shown in the following examples.

Objective: Fund-raiser/Development Associate with a nonprofit or educational institution that will benefit from proven strengths in sales and relationship management.

Goal: Entry into the Acme Management Training program as the first step in a fulfilling career in the Supply Chain Management field.

Target: Career as **MECHANICAL ENGINEER** in the aerospace industry, applying creative skills and technical problem-solving to advance the state of the art.

Seeking position as a **Project Coordinator** for a commercial construction firm.

30-Minute Resume Makeover

Now that you've reviewed the pros, cons, and other considerations for creating a powerful Summary to introduce your resume, take 30 minutes to edit and improve your current version. Be sure you incorporate the key points from this section:

- Clearly communicate who you are and the value you offer.

- Include keywords.

- Communicate your personal brand.

- Highlight your "wow" achievements.

- If you decide an Objective is the right strategy for you, write one that is clearly focused and communicates what you will bring to the company, not just what you want.

STRATEGY #3: Emphasize Experience and Accomplishments

When writing their resumes, many people make the mistake of placing too much emphasis on their job descriptions. In fact, they go into a great deal of detail about their day-to-day activities and job responsibilities, thinking that they must demonstrate they are familiar with every aspect of the job they are applying for.

A key problem with this approach is that the resume reads like a job description, not a unique and powerful presentation of capabilities. And it makes one resume sound much like another, assuming candidates have held similar jobs; no one stands out.

In reality, employers don't care much about job descriptions. What they care about is what you have done while holding that job. Your resume, then, should showcase the unique contributions you have made to your past employers, teammates, and projects.

Employers also want to know where you've worked—the names and locations of your employers, your dates of employment, and a bit about what the company does. Here is an illustration of a logical format for presenting this information:

COMPANY NAME, city, state   Date employment started–Date ended

Brief description of the company: how large it is, what it does, who it serves

Most Recent Job Title (add dates if you held more than one job with this company)

Brief description of the scope of your job and key challenges or circumstances that existed when you took the job.

- Accomplishment

- Accomplishment

- Accomplishment

- Accomplishment

(continued)

(continued)

Prior Job Title (with dates)

Brief description of the scope of your job and key challenges or circumstances that existed when you took the job.

- Accomplishment

- Accomplishment

- Accomplishment

In listing your dates of employment, you might choose to use months and years (April 2004 to October 2007) or simply years (2004–2007). There are two advantages to using years only: It is cleaner and less cluttered, and it can disguise short employment gaps. You will probably be asked to use months and years in job applications, so be sure to keep these dates handy if you don't use them in your resume.

With your material well organized, you can move on to creating the content that will lift your resume to the top of the pile—high-impact position descriptions and powerful achievements that position you as a top performer.

Write High-Impact Position Descriptions

I've just said that employers don't care much about position descriptions. Yet you do need to provide *some* detail about your various positions—your scope of responsibility, major functions, budget numbers, staff reporting relationships, and so forth. Still, there's no need to make these position descriptions dry and boring, and there's certainly no need to write lengthy, detailed accounts of your daily activities.

Tips for High-Impact Position Descriptions

Here's how to make these sections sing:

- Give a big-picture overview of your general scope of responsibility, not a minute list of daily job duties.

- Use active verbs to describe what you do rather than passive "responsible for" statements.

- Remember that you will be describing some of your activities in your accomplishment statements, and you'll have the chance to include appropriate keywords there. For example, if you're a marketing manager and part of your job is to manage the company's trade show activity, you don't need to detail this in your position descriptions if one of your bullet points states, "Created new system for trade show follow-up that boosted after-show sales by 57%."

- Consider describing the particular challenge you faced or task you were given when taking each job. Given this context information, readers will be even more impressed with the results you were able to attain.

- Think about the one most important thing you did in each job and write a powerful summary statement to lead off each position description. Why not put this sentence in bold type so that anyone quickly skimming the resume will capture the most significant contributions of your career?

The following three examples illustrate powerful openings and concise position descriptions.

For a hotel general manager:

> Reversed negative profit performance and stemmed decline of aging hotel in a competitive business/tourism market. Managed P&L and annual business plan to achieve performance objectives. Led a team of 9 operational supervisors and 3 sales managers.

For a manufacturing operations manager:

> Turned around unprofitable business unit, aggressively applying Lean Manufacturing and Six Sigma methodologies to reduce costs and increase productivity and profitability in a QS 9000 production environment. Managed P&L, new business development, product development, manufacturing engineering, strategic planning, and sales forecasting for $60M, 300-employee division producing climate-control systems for major automotive accounts.

For a sales manager:

> Led 12-member National Accounts team to exceed 100% of aggressive goals, selling to and servicing large corporate customers in 8-state Northeast region. Managed sales reporting, staff assignments, and expense budgets. Set individual sales objectives, created motivational sales contests, and worked with sales reps to improve selling skills.

Remember to restrain your position descriptions to no more than four or five lines. If you need to say more, break up the text into two paragraphs.

Make Powerful Achievements the Focal Point

Now it's time to write about what really matters! Because your accomplishments are the most interesting and important part of your resume, they should be the focal point. You want employers to notice them immediately, grasp their significance, appreciate their value, and translate your past accomplishments to future performance at their company.

Wow. That's a lot to ask. But the following format and content recommendations will help you to appropriately emphasize your achievements and create a unique and compelling resume.

Before we look at some examples, let's address what may be the greatest challenge for most resume writers: coming up with the accomplishments to put on your resume.

If you're like most people, you've experienced varying levels of success throughout your career. Sometimes you're the home-run champ and other times you're a "utility player," turning in a solid performance day after day but not putting up showy statistics. For some positions, you might not remember (or maybe never knew) the specific results you achieved.

How, then, do you write accomplishment statements that will knock the socks off employers?

Tips to Identify and Present Your Accomplishments

This three-part exercise guides you through the process of creating accomplishment statements that are meaningful, relevant, and will present you in the best possible light.

1. First, understand the kinds of accomplishments that are meaningful to employers:

   - **Making money** (increasing revenue and/or profits, increasing productivity)

   - **Saving money** (cutting costs, reducing waste, eliminating inefficiency)

- **Expanding business** (attracting new customers, more customers, better customers; increasing business with existing customers; entering new markets; boosting market share)

- **Saving time** (increasing efficiency, streamlining processes, eliminating unnecessary activities, restructuring work flow)

- **Retaining customers, business relationships, and employees**

- **Building company visibility, image, and brand value**

- **Solving problems** (resolving issues that prevent any of the above good things from happening)

2. Use the following prompts to identify your relevant experiences and key successes—the raw material for your accomplishment statements.

   For each position you've held, and perhaps your outside-of-work activities as well, ask yourself these questions:

   - What was I expected to do? Did I have specific performance goals, and if so, did I meet or exceed them?

   - Did I make money for the company?

   - Did I save money or time?

   - Did I expand the business?

   - Did I retain customers, business relationships, or employees?

   - Did I build company visibility, image, or brand value?

   - What problems did I solve?

   - What was going on in my department, the company, the industry, or the economy? What obstacles might have prevented me from reaching my goals?

   - How did I compare to my peers?

   - How did my performance compare to industry averages?

3. From your raw material, write accomplishment statements for each position following these guidelines:

   - Describe each specific achievement in a separate bullet point.

   - Include numbers and hard results whenever possible—dollars, percentages, and comparisons. These add meaning, credibility, and distinctiveness to your resume.

- Keep your statements crisp, preferably no more than two or three lines.

- Add just enough context information to put readers "in the picture" without drowning them with detail.

- Look for ways to make your accomplishments visually distinctive. You might highlight numbers and keywords in bold type, or get creative with tables, charts, graphs, or other visuals that will grab the reader's attention and focus it precisely where you want it—on your areas of greatest performance.

In the following resume excerpts, notice how accomplishments are the focal point—strong, compelling, and visually distinctive.

FARFLUNG FOOD, Cleves, OH   2006–2008
$40M food-service provider to offshore and land-based facilities
GENERAL MANAGER

Revitalized the company. Stepping into interim "rescue" assignment, preserved key contracts, improved financial and operational performance, increased customer satisfaction, and created strategic and tactical blueprints for continued success and growth of the company.

☑ Retained 2 major accounts—**23%** of total sales volume—by boosting visibility, customer contact, and customer service.
☑ Swiftly reduced food costs **2%** and administrative labor expenses **3.5%** by introducing accurate expense-monitoring systems.
☑ Increased client satisfaction level from **60%** to **93%.**
☑ Turned around lackluster financial organization, reengineered the internal-controls structure, and created a smooth-functioning unit supporting **23** clients in **119** locations.
☑ Enhanced training, communication, staff selection, and performance.

XAVIER TECHNOLOGIES ($700M global test and measurement company), Boston, MA 2005–Present

BUSINESS MANAGER / NEW BUSINESS PRODUCT MANAGER

Hired to develop and implement sales and marketing programs to capitalize on new business opportunities. Concurrently, challenged to improve performance of existing multimillion-dollar product line and resolve sales efficiency barriers.

- Developed new business model for innovative technology to generate $20M incremental business in 3 years—$100K revenue and $1M+ sales funnel in first 3 months.

- Drove product-line optimization that delivered 42% profit growth during severe industry downturn:

	2005	2006	2007	2008
Revenue	$6.5M	$5M	$5M	$5.5M
Gross Margin	28%	60%	70%	70%

- Developed a Web-based configuration / quote tool for the global sales team that reduced customer quote times from 3 days to 15 minutes.

Medi-Test, Inc.   Chicago, IL, 2004–2007
DIRECTOR OF PRODUCT DEVELOPMENT, SALES, AND MARKETING
Drove explosive growth to #1 brand in its category. Led pioneering product development and
aggressive sales and marketing to lift company to position of market dominance.

- Delivered 350%+ revenue growth in 30 months.
- Identified market niches, overhauled product line and packaging, and led re-launch that established Medi-Test as the leading brand at retail.
- Significantly expanded placements, adding 50,000+ shelf facings at major retailers including Target and Kroger.
- Created an entirely new category and shepherded pioneering product through FDA approval.

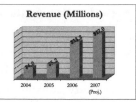
Revenue (Millions)
2004 2005 2006 2007 (Proj.)

Incorporating Your Accomplishments into a Functional Resume

Even if you plan to use a functional format, I recommend that you take the time to explore each of your past positions and other experiences and write specific accomplishment statements for each. This is the best way to organize your material before you regroup it under functional headings.

To prepare your functional achievement section, look at the core competencies needed for your target jobs. Next, group your relevant accomplishments under each competency area. Create keyword-rich headings that will create the right perception. For example, the functional resume for Barbara Jenner (page 76) uses the following headings that are a perfect fit for Barbara's target job of Fund-raiser/Development Associate:

- Fund-raising/Event Planning
- Relationship Management
- Project Management
- Organizational Improvement

Your experience and accomplishments should be the meatiest part of your resume—the entrée, if you will, between the "appetizer" (the Summary) and the "dessert" (the "Extras" that will follow). Take the time to delve back through your career and come up with a hearty portion of specific examples, numbers, and results that will please employers looking for a rich, substantial addition to their talent pool.

30-Minute Resume Makeover

For each position included on your resume, review the following tips to be certain you are communicating just enough of the right information.

- Briefly describe the scope of each position without getting bogged down in the minutiae of your day-to-day activities.

- Understand what's meaningful to employers (making money, saving money, expanding business, saving time, retaining business, building visibility, solving problems) and come up with specific examples of how you have done that for past employers.

- Quantify, quantify, quantify! Use comparisons, dollars, percentages, and other measurable results to prove you delivered value.

- Spice up the visual presentation of your accomplishments with charts, graphs, and tables.

- Make sure the accomplishments are crisp, easy to read, and as compelling as possible.

STRATEGY #4: Enhance with Education and "Extras"

After the intensive work you've just done to describe your experience and accomplishments, it's time to take a breather! Fortunately, the Education and "Extras" sections of your resume are typically the fastest and easiest to write. There are just a few things you'll want to consider as you prepare these sections.

Presenting Your Education

If you have the textbook educational qualifications for your target jobs, great! For most professional and managerial roles, this means a bachelor's degree in a relevant field of study and perhaps an advanced degree in business, management, or your specific discipline.

Unless your education is very recent, place this section towards the end of your resume; it does not need to be a focal point but merely a credential that the employer can readily check.

If you are a new graduate looking for your first professional job, your education might be one of your most important qualifications and, as such, should appear in a more prominent position on your resume—perhaps immediately after your Summary.

If you returned to school mid-career to earn or finish a degree, I recommend keeping your experience and accomplishments as the focal point and positioning the education towards the end. Of course, if you are changing careers and earned a degree or certification that is a prime requirement for your new field, you would follow the advice for other new graduates.

As a rule, include your year of graduation unless you are concerned about revealing your age. It's perfectly all right to omit the graduation date.

In a nutshell, you want to let employers know you have the educational credentials they require. They don't need to know a great deal about your college activities, coursework, or other experiences unless you are using these as a primary qualification (again, most likely for new grads). So keep it simple with a brief, easy-to-skim Education section, as shown in the following examples.

Just the facts:

THE OHIO STATE UNIVERSITY, Columbus, OH
BS, Business Administration, magna cum laude, 1998

Executive education:

MBA—Graduate School of Management, **Northwestern University**
BA Political Science—**Dartmouth College**
Executive education—**American Management Association, Harvard Business School**

Recent grad:

Boston College, Chestnut Hill, MA
Bachelor of Arts in English, 2008

- 3.6 GPA; Dean's List all semesters
- Four-year varsity tennis player; Team Captain, 2007–2008
- Secretary of Student Association, 2006–2008

Non-degree certifications:

Registered Phlebotomist, State of Arizona, 2006
Certified Nursing Assistant, University of Arizona, 1990
Certified Nursing Aide, State of Arizona, 1988

Obviously, a lack of formal education has not stopped many people from excelling in their careers. The world's most successful college dropout may be Bill Gates, who left school to found Microsoft! Maybe you, too, stopped short before completing your degree, or took some college courses but never pursued a degree full time. Perhaps you graduated from the "school of hard knocks" and have no college education at all.

> **Tip:** If at all possible, include keywords such as "BS degree," "Bachelor's Degree," "business administration," and other terms relevant to your profession; this may help you to get past automated resume screeners.

Don't let this stop you from pursuing your goals. Within your resume, focus on your experience and accomplishments while making your education section as strong as it (truthfully) can be. Here are some ways to do that:

UNIVERSITY OF IDAHO, Moscow, ID
Completed 75% of requirements for BS degree in Marketing.

UNIVERSITY OF CALIFORNIA, Los Angeles, CA
Completed 100+ hours of continuing professional education while working 45+ hours per week. Studied marketing, sales, business administration, customer relationship management, finance, and accounting.

Adding the "Extras"

Many job seekers want to share qualifications, experiences, activities, or other information about themselves that doesn't fit into the three main sections of the resume (Summary, Experience, and Education) but that add depth and richness to the overall picture.

Possible "Extras" for Your Resume

These "Extras" can not only round out your qualifications, they can tell employers more about you as a person and as a professional. While they should not overwhelm the rest of the resume, these "Extras" can be a valuable addition.

- Proficiency in multiple languages

- Technology skills and proficiencies

- Extensive international travel, work, or study

- Publications you've written—books, articles, theses, or white papers

- News stories in which you were quoted or profiled

- Presentations and public speaking experiences

- Professional affiliations and any leadership roles, committees, task forces, or special assignments within those associations

- Volunteer activities and civic affiliations

- Personal information, such as interests and activities, organizations, and athletic pursuits

The following examples will give you some ideas for how to format and present this information in your resume.

————————————————ADDITIONAL INFORMATION————————————————

Study Abroad: Tokyo International University, Kawagoe, Japan

Language Skills: Basic Japanese and Basic Spanish

Publication: "An American in Tokyo: Survival Strategies for International Students," *Northeastern Today* campus newspaper

Computer Competencies: Excel, Word, WordPerfect, Outlook, PowerPoint, Internet, Westlaw, LexisNexis, Summation, MPID, TimeWriter, GroupWise

---

Memberships/Community Service

Active Member, Western Washington University Accounting Society
Co-Founder and Treasurer, Hamlet Railway Museum—*new nonprofit association*
Volunteer, Habitat for Humanity

Be selective about what you include and don't let the "Extras" outweigh your professional qualifications.

Before concluding the "Education and Extras" strategy, let's quickly review a list of elements that should *not* appear in your resume—for all kinds of reasons, such as legal hiring guidelines, privacy concerns, and simply because they are inappropriate or unnecessary.

What Not to Include in Your Resume

Here are some things it's better to leave out:

- **Salary information:** It's not beneficial to you to share this information in your resume—or, in fact, at any point prior to a formal job offer being made. Keep it to yourself and negotiate your new salary based on your value to the organization, not your past pay.

- **Reasons for leaving:** I don't recommend that you take up valuable space on your resume with this non-essential information. Most employers will ask during the interview, so do be prepared to answer the question.

- **Supervisor's name:** At this stage of the process, employers do not need to know the name of the individual you reported to.

- **Photographs:** A photograph is not only unnecessary, it could reveal information about your age, gender, race, or ethnicity that employers would prefer not to have because of the need to comply with legal hiring guidelines.

- **Personal information:** Keep your private information private! Your date of birth, social security number, and details about your marital status, number of children, religious affiliations, and most hobbies should be omitted from your resume.

- **"References upon request":** It's not necessary to add this line to your resume; employers assume you will provide references if asked.

30-Minute Resume Makeover

As you review your Education and Extras, make sure they enhance your resume and don't detract from the powerful and cohesive message you are trying to convey. Here are the top tips:

- Keep these sections crisp and concise, including just the information that is relevant and appropriate.

- It is critical to use educational keywords such as BS or bachelor's degree to avoid being screened out by automated resume scanners. If you have one or more degrees, be sure to list them using standard terminology. If you don't, try to include the keywords without misleading readers about your educational credentials (as illustrated in the examples).

- Include continuing education, as appropriate, to enhance your Education section.

- Unless you are a new grad, don't add details of your college experience to your Education section.

- Consider adding "Extras" that round out the picture of who you are and what makes you unique.

- Don't include inappropriate, unnecessary, personal, or private information on your resume.

STRATEGY #5: Proofread and Polish to Perfection

Seldom is the first draft of a resume the final copy. Even experienced writers who have written thousands of resumes need to trim, edit, wordsmith, shape, and polish every first draft to achieve a winning result—a resume that is on target, compelling, and as perfect as possible.

It's helpful to take a breather before moving on to the proofreading and polishing stage. When you come back, you'll look at your draft with fresh eyes and be able to be more accurate and more objective in correcting and tweaking it.

So—take a break! Let your draft simmer while your ideas percolate and your thoughts clarify. When you're ready to start again, chapter 3 will lead you through the steps to proofread and polish your resume.

Key Points: Chapter 2

- Choose the appropriate structure for your resume (chronological/hybrid or functional) and organize the material for logical flow from top to bottom.

- Design and format your resume to draw attention to key information and to create an attractive document that is easy to read.

- Create a strong summary that includes the relevant keywords for your profession.

- Distinguish your resume by including a personal brand statement and your "wow" achievements.

- Write high-impact position descriptions, not boring summaries of "job responsibilities."

- Make powerful and specific achievement statements the focal point. Use comparisons, dollars, percentages, and other measurable results to prove that you delivered value for past employers.

- Present your education credentials in a concise, easy-to-check format.

- Add "Extras" that enhance the overall portrait you are painting in you resume.

Chapter 3

Proofread and Polish to Perfection

With the hard work of writing the first-draft copy of your resume complete, it's time to polish that rough gem into a shining jewel. In this chapter I lay out a process that you can follow to improve both the content and the appearance of your final resume. I recommend that you go through the entire process at least twice, continuing to refine the document until it is practically perfect.

In this chapter you'll also find step-by-step instructions for converting your resume to the text-only format you'll need for electronic applications.

Review Your Content

If you took my recommendation at the end of chapter 2, you put your resume away to "breathe" for a short while before beginning to proofread and polish. It's amazing how even a brief absence makes your eye and ear sharper, so you'll be able to find errors, inconsistencies, and awkward language on a quick read-through. Follow these steps to ensure your resume is on target:

1. Revisit your current career goal so that it is fresh in your mind.

2. Read your resume slowly and carefully, thinking solely whether each section, paragraph, bullet point, and phrase supports your goal. Edit content as necessary to align with your objective.

3. Read your resume again, this time looking for errors—misspellings, incorrect word choices, poor grammar, and incorrect use of punctuation.

4. Now review your resume looking for inconsistencies. Are all the headings the same size and style? Is spacing between sections consistent? Have you used type enhancements consistently? Is the type style and size the same in all sections?

5. Finally, after you've completed your edits, run a spell-check to be sure you haven't overlooked any misspellings. I recommend that you do this *last* rather than *first* because it's all too easy to introduce an error during the editing process, and if you think you've already completed the spell-check you might not notice the error.

Design (or Redesign) Your Document

Some people like to design as they go along, while others prefer to get the content down first, then play with the layout. Either method works fine. But even if you've predetermined your design, go through the following review steps to be sure your document is making the very best impression:

1. Choose a widely accepted font (Arial, Arial Narrow, Book Antiqua, Bookman, Garamond, Georgia, Tahoma, Times New Roman, or Verdana) in a readable size—generally 10 or 11 point.

2. Accentuate headings and subheadings with larger type in bold and/or italics.

3. Use bold type to accentuate key information—perhaps your job titles, company names, achievements, or the numbers in your achievement statements.

4. Make sure there is adequate white space between sections of your resume, between paragraphs, and possibly between bullet points.

5. Review all of your paragraphs and bullet points. Do any of them exceed four or five lines? If so, and especially if *several* of them are lengthy, take one or more of these steps to reduce them to a more readable length:

   • Edit to trim the length of the copy.

   • Break long paragraphs into two.

   • Reduce the size of your font.

   • Make your left and right margins a bit smaller to accommodate paragraphs on fewer lines.

6. Review your lists of bullet points. Do any of them exceed five or six? If so, review to be sure all the items are necessary, and decide if you want to add subheadings or some other division to break up the long list.

7. Check your page breaks. It may be necessary to adjust your layout or content if the page break occurs at an awkward place.

8. If your resume is longer than one page, add a header on the top of page 2 that includes your name and preferably some contact information (your e-mail address and phone), just in case the two pages get separated.

9. Run spell-check again to be sure you didn't introduce any errors during the editing process.

Red Flag Review

Conduct a final check of your resume to be sure you haven't inadvertently highlighted any information that will cause a "red-flag" reaction by employers. As stated in chapter 1, any of the following could raise questions in the employer's mind:

- Long gaps between employment
- Many short-term jobs ("job hopping")
- An erratic career track—veering from one field to another without apparent purpose
- Lack of evidence that you performed well on the job
- Demotion
- Too much time in the same job
- Misspellings, poor grammar, poor writing, or obvious errors
- Resumes that are too long (3+ pages)
- Resumes that lack substance
- Functional resumes that don't make it clear when and where you acquired your skills and experience

Should you find any red-flag items, see what you can do to minimize their appearance, so that they are not the first or the most important points that catch the reader's attention.

Get a Second Opinion

It's always worthwhile to have a trusted friend or your spouse or partner look at your resume. They might not have deep experience about your profession, but they can spot errors and inconsistencies and let you know whether the resume is a good reflection of the person they know so well.

Even better, enlist a professional colleague, such as a co-worker, your mentor, a prior boss, or member of your professional association, to review your document. These people have deep knowledge of your field, your industry, and perhaps your career. They can give you an informed opinion as to whether you've created a meaningful and compelling document or sold yourself short.

Be prepared, though, for some criticism and nitpicky comments. You will have to be the judge of whether their suggestions make sense, based on your current goals and the strategies you applied in creating your resume. Whether or not you adopt all their suggestions, let them know that you sincerely appreciate their help.

Finalize Your Document

With all of your edits and corrections made, the final step in preparing your resume is to e-mail the Word document to a couple of friends. Ask them if they experienced any glitches in receiving, viewing, or printing your resume. Was the pagination okay? Did the font come through perfectly? Because you'll be e-mailing your resume to employers and network contacts throughout your search, you want to minimize any technical problems.

Although e-mail will probably be your dominant means of transmitting your resume, you will still have a need for nicely printed copies. You can bring them on interviews, share them during networking meetings, and even on occasion mail them in response to opportunities you uncover.

Stock up on a good-quality resume paper that you can find through office supply firms. Choose a conservative, professional color, such as white, ivory or cream, light gray, or light blue, in a finish you like. You want your printed resume to continue the professional image you have established for yourself in your resume content and in all of the experiences of your career.

There's no need to stockpile printed resumes. Just create half a dozen good sets to have on hand for when you're in a hurry or have a sudden opportunity. You can print more as the need arises.

Convert Your Resume to Text Format

If you've ever tried to cut-and-paste a formatted Word resume into an online application, you know what can happen to all of your careful formatting! Although automated systems are becoming increasingly sophisticated and able to read a variety of formats, don't take the chance that your great content will be corrupted or lost before your resume reaches the employer.

Simply, you'll want to create a text-only version of your resume and you can cut-and-paste without incident.

The text-only format, also called ASCII text, is universally readable on any computer. It takes away all of the beautiful font and format enhancements that add so much to the visual presentation and readability of most resumes. But it makes that document very computer-friendly and fully scannable by any automated system.

Follow these steps to create a text-only version of your resume:

1. Create a new version of your resume using the "Save As" feature of your word-processing program. Select "plain text"/"text only" or "ASCII" in the "Save As" option box.

2. Close the new file.

3. Reopen the file, and you'll find that your word processor has automatically reformatted your resume into a common font, such as Courier, removed all formatting, and left-justified the text.

4. Review the resume and fix any "glitches" such as odd characters that may have been inserted to take the place of "curly" quotes, dashes, accents, or other nonstandard symbols.

5. If necessary, add extra blank lines to improve readability.

6. Consider adding horizontal dividers to break the resume into sections for improved skimmability. You can use any standard typewriter symbols such as *, -, (,), =, +, ^, or #.

To illustrate what you can expect when creating the text version of your resume, compare this sample resume, presented in both standard (Microsoft Word) format and text-only.

Sean L. Thomas, CPA

7529 Beech Avenue, Naperville, IL 60564
(847) 555-1234 • seanthomas@yahoo.com

ACCOUNTING MANAGER / FINANCIAL ANALYST

Finance professional with a track record of cost savings and tight fiscal administration in both corporate and manufacturing environments. Verifiable accomplishments in corporate finance, plant accounting (both start-up and ongoing), and automated systems implementation.

Results-focused manager with proven ability to strategize, create project plans, implement, and follow through to completion. Effective communicator, skilled at gaining team support for key projects. Rapidly productive in new environments.

PROFESSIONAL EXPERIENCE

PLANET INDUSTRIES, INC., Detroit, MI, 2000–Present
Global manufacturer of plastic films, aluminum extrusions, and vinyl extrusions.

Accounting Manager, 2005–Present   *Plant Start-up, Evanston, IL*
Established all financial systems and controls for new manufacturing operation. Provided financial oversight during growth to $60 million in annual sales, with monthly operating budget of $700K.

- Spearheaded project to implement Oracle ERP system. Oversaw in-house customization of software, system documentation, initial implementation and testing, and ongoing training to ensure active and appropriate use throughout the organization. Project completed on schedule and 5% under budget.

- Piloted an activity-based accounting program and prepared numerous cost / benefit analyses. Identified opportunities for increased efficiency and reduced operating costs, successfully quantifying criteria for capital projects.

Project Analyst, Fixed Assets, 2002–2005   *Corporate Headquarters, Detroit, MI*

- Implemented a fixed asset component to the company's mainframe system. Served as key project coordinator, tracking and documenting team activities to ensure successful completion— 3 weeks ahead of schedule, meeting all budget and performance parameters.

Staff Accountant, 2000–2002   *Corporate Headquarters, Detroit, MI*

- Performed cost accounting, budgeting, capital budget preparation, month-end closing, P&L statements, and full spectrum of corporate accounting functions.

PRIOR EXPERIENCE
- **Manager of Financial Reporting,** Concordia College, Ann Arbor, MI, 1998–2000
- **Fixed Asset Accountant,** GPA Packaging, Detroit, MI, 1997–1998
- **Cost / Budget Accountant,** Vinyl Corporation, Detroit, MI, 1994–1997

EDUCATION AND CERTIFICATION

B.S. Accounting, 1994: University of Michigan, Ann Arbor, MI
CPA certification, 1998

Figure 3.1: A standard-format resume.

```
SEAN L. THOMAS, CPA
7529 Beech Avenue, Naperville, IL 60564
(847) 555-1234 * seanthomas@yahoo.com

==========================================
ACCOUNTING MANAGER / FINANCIAL ANALYST

Finance professional with a track record of cost savings and tight fiscal
administration in both corporate and manufacturing environments. Verifiable
accomplishments in corporate finance, plant accounting (both start-up and
ongoing), and automated systems implementation.

Results-focused manager with proven ability to strategize, create project plans,
implement, and follow through to completion. Effective communicator, skilled at
gaining team support for key projects. Rapidly productive in new environments.

==========================================
PROFESSIONAL EXPERIENCE

PLANET INDUSTRIES, INC., Detroit, MI, 2000-Present
Global manufacturer of plastic films, aluminum extrusions, and vinyl extrusions.

Accounting Manager, 2005-Present - Plant Start-up, Evanston, IL
-------------------------------------------
Established all financial systems and controls for new manufacturing operation.
Provided financial oversight during growth to $60 million in annual sales, with
monthly operating budget of $700K.

* Spearheaded project to implement Oracle ERP system. Oversaw in-house
customization of software, system documentation, initial implementation and
testing, and ongoing training to ensure active and appropriate use throughout the
organization. Project completed on schedule and 5% under budget.
* Piloted an activity-based accounting program and prepared numerous cost /
benefit analyses. Identified opportunities for increased efficiency and reduced
operating costs, successfully quantifying criteria for capital projects.

Project Analyst, Fixed Assets, 2002-2005 - Corporate Headquarters, Detroit, MI
-------------------------------------------
* Implemented a fixed asset component to the company's mainframe system. Served
as key project coordinator, tracking and documenting team activities to ensure
successful completion--3 weeks ahead of schedule, meeting all budget and
performance parameters.

Staff Accountant, 2000-2002 - Corporate Headquarters, Detroit, MI
-------------------------------------------
* Performed cost accounting, budgeting, capital budget preparation, month-end
closing, P&L statements, and full spectrum of corporate accounting functions.

PRIOR EXPERIENCE
* Manager of Financial Reporting, Concordia College, Ann Arbor, MI, 1998-2000
* Fixed Asset Accountant, GPA Packaging, Detroit, MI, 1997-1998
* Cost / Budget Accountant, Vinyl Corporation, Detroit, MI, 1994-1997

==========================================
EDUCATION AND CERTIFICATION

B.S. Accounting, 1994: University of Michigan, Ann Arbor, MI
CPA certification, 1998
```

Figure 3.2: A text-only resume.

Makeover Complete...Now What?

With these final steps, you've completed your 30-Minute Resume Makeover. You should have a concise, targeted, relevant, and effective resume that answers employers' questions and positions you perfectly for your dream job.

So now what? To put your new resume to use, you'll need to prepare cover letters (chapter 5) and conduct an effective search (chapter 6). It might be fun to review the before-and-after resume makeovers in the next chapter before plunging into the next challenge.

Key Points: Chapter 3

- Revisit your content to be sure it supports your current career goals.
- Review all material for accuracy and consistency.
- Design your resume for readability.
- Recheck for employer "red flags."
- Get a second opinion from trusted colleagues.
- Create a final document that e-mails and prints to perfection.
- Convert your resume to text format for online applications.

Chapter 4

Before-and-After Resume Transformations

Sure, it's helpful to look at a gallery of great resumes as you work on your 30-Minute Resume Makeover. But sometimes it's even more beneficial to compare, side by side, before-and-after versions of the same resume so you can see what a difference strategy, format, and content make in changing a resume from ineffective to effective.

In this chapter I share with you 18 resume makeovers, as executed by professional resume writers, all recent graduates of the Resume Writing Academy. In the narrative that accompanies each set of resumes, you can read about the specific challenges faced by the writer and how she addressed them. What's more, you'll see how each of the five Resume Makeover Strategies is applied to make the "after" version a compelling and effective document that supports the objectives of that particular job seeker.

Resume Transformation #1: Patrick J. Kelly

Resume Writer:

Ilona Vanderwoude, CPRW, CCMC, CEIP, CJST
Career Branches
P.O. Box 330
Riverdale, NY 10471
Phone: (718) 884-2213
E-mail: ilona@CareerBranches.com
www.CareerBranches.com

The Situation

Patrick had not held paid employment for more than ten years. In the interim, he had been active in a variety of unpaid roles as a talent manager, speaker, and trainer for nonprofit organizations and his own entrepreneurial ventures. Now he wanted to pull together all of his diverse experiences to position himself as a corporate trainer with expertise in teaching communication skills.

The "Before" Version

Beginning with an objective and proceeding through a reverse-chronological presentation of Patrick's various activities, the original resume was bland in appearance and in content. It contained no compelling information—nothing to make readers believe in Patrick's ability to train others and to lead complex programs to execution. Going back more than 25 years, the resume contained no quantifiable achievements.

The "After" Version—Applying the Five Resume Makeover Strategies

- **Fashion a Strong Framework.** A hybrid format was chosen to pull relevant information up front. In fact, this resume includes a short functional section, titled "Core Expertise & Achievements," that emphasizes Patrick's strongest and most relevant experience. The reverse-chronological career history is broken down into "Related Experience," which emphasizes Patrick's recent unpaid activities, and "Early Career Development," a section without dates that allows the inclusion of a few specific accomplishments and name-dropping of some prominent Broadway musicals.

- **Start with a Superlative Summary.** A bold headline and "raising the bar" personal brand statement instantly communicate Patrick's expertise and his passion for excellence. Keywords for his target field of training and communications are used liberally throughout the summary and in a special keyword section titled "Key Areas of Strength."

- **Emphasize Experience and Accomplishments.** Each position, whether paid or unpaid, includes a concise description containing only the details that are relevant to his current goal. Where possible, accomplishments are quantified, and bold type is used to accent his key successes.

- **Enhance with Education and "Extras."** Patrick has a strong educational background, with a master's degree in Speech and Theater and a bachelor's degree in Speech, English, and Media Arts. The resume includes an appropriate Education section, and Patrick's master's degree is also mentioned in the Summary, which also contains a brief "Extra" regarding his ability to travel.

● **Proofread and Polish to Perfection.** The sharp format and well-written content enhance the message that Patrick wants to convey about being an expert communicator and trainer.

Patrick J. Kelly
86 Redstone Road
Danbury, CT 06810

Work 214-905-7888   Cell 203-911-9073

pkelly@kelly.com

Objective	A responsible position in coordinating speaker engagements and/or training speakers

Experience

Neutral Ground
Program Committee Member
Actively seek speakers and coordinate arrangements from booking to
actual engagement. Arrange speaking programs for the organization.
Danbury, CT
2004-Present

Communication For Everyone
Founder and Director
Created company providing professional and management training in
communication and negotiation skills, interviewer training, and presentation
techniques.
Danbury, CT
2000-2004

Patrick Kelly Productions
Talent Manager and Producer
Handled all public relations, publicity, and funding for individual clients.
Obtained bookings and negotiated contracts. Prepared clients for performances.
Danbury, CT
1994-2000

Young Athletes Foundation
Speaker's Bureau Coordinator
As full-time consultant, obtained, negotiated, and coordinated engagements for
prominent young athletes to speak at corporations, colleges, and other events.
Stamford, CT
April-Dec. 1998

Susan Bergman, Producer and Composer
Co-producer
Coordinated production staff for *Hairspray, Into the Woods,* and
Jekyll & Hyde, Arranged publicity and directed fund-raising efforts.
New York, NY
1995-1997

Parent Teachers Association
Liaison and Committee Chair
Coordinated fund-raising events and chaired major committees.
New Rochelle, NY
1980-1992

Adriatic Cruises
Cruise Consultant
Gave seminars and sold cruises to individuals and groups.
Yonkers, NY
1990-1995

Jill McNulty & Associates
Co-Director of Advertising
Radio Advertising Researcher and Salesperson.
New York, NY
1987-1990

Green Apple Barter Services
Account Executive
Expanded customer base by selling memberships to bartering partners.
New York, NY
1985-1986

St. Barnabas High School
Teacher
Teacher of Speech, English, Theater, and Media Arts.
New York, NY
1980-1985

Skills
Exceptional marketing, organizational, and negotiation skills.
Excellent coach for presentations to audiences and media.

Education
Baruch College: BA, Speech, English, and Media Arts
Baruch College: MA, Speech and Theater

Figure 4.1: Before.

PATRICK J. KELLY

86 Redstone Road ▪ Danbury, CT 06810
H: 203.325.9951 ▪ C: 203.911.9073 ▪ pkelly@kelly.com

Executive Training–Workshops–Presentations–Fortune 500–Speakers Bureau Training

COMMUNICATIONS & TRAINING SPECIALIST
Raising the Bar for Performance, Productivity, and Profits

Driving effectiveness of individuals and organizations by delivering communication skills training to broad audiences, including executives and sales staff. More than 15-year track record of **setting new standards and getting people to perform, consistently achieving "the impossible"** with regard to booking high-profile speakers, reaching sales goals, and succeeding where others fail. Training expertise in persuasive speaking, negotiations, sales, and public speaking in one-on-one and group settings, achieving measurable skills improvement. Outstanding public speaking and sales skills: prospecting, negotiating, and closing deals.

Master's degree in Speech and Theater. Valid driver's license and availability to travel.

Key Areas of Strength

Executive Presentation Skills	Process Streamlining	Talent Management/Production
Professional Development	PR/Media Management	Sales Presentation/Negotiation
Persuasive Speaking	Speech Coaching	Consultative Selling Skills

CORE EXPERTISE & ACHIEVEMENTS

Executive Training

- Trained Fortune 500 executives in boardroom presentations, employee and stakeholder communications, and media relations.

Negotiations, Sales & Persuasive Speaking/Training

- Conducting sales seminars in one-on-one and group environments of up to 50; sales improved 35% within the next few months.

Public Speaking/Workshops/Seminars

- Presenting lectures on topics including health, business, and government affairs for broad range of audiences: corporate, academic, and non-profit.

RELATED EXPERIENCE

Communication For Everyone, Danbury, CT, 2000 to Present
FOUNDER & DIRECTOR

Provide professional and management training with emphasis on communication and negotiation skills, interview training, and presentation techniques. Develop speaking programs, identify speakers, and coordinate arrangements.

- **Delivered presentations for large membership of "Neutral Ground" and audiences of up to 100** on topics such as health, career change, college admission, and interview preparation.

Patrick Kelly Productions, Danbury, CT, 1994 to 2000
TALENT MANAGER & PRODUCER

Founded and operated consulting firm specializing in career development and job/project placement for cabaret artists. Organized career fairs.

- Managed all public relations, publicity, and funding for individual clients.
- **Secured bookings, negotiated contracts, and prepared clients for performances,** achieving success rate 60% above peer average.

Figure 4.2: After.

PATRICK J. KELLY   C: 203.911.9073 ▪ pkelly@kelly.com ▪ Page 2 of 2

Young Athletes Foundation, Stamford, CT, 1998
HEAD OF SPEAKERS' BUREAU
Hired as consultant for 8-month assignment. Rapidly mastered new field without prior sports knowledge or experience. Identified, approached, secured, negotiated, and coordinated speaking engagements at events and at colleges, non-profits, and large corporations for prominent young athletes. Developed fund-raising events.

- **Pioneered speaker training for young athletes to increase foundation's revenues:**
  – Trained athletes one-on-one and in groups to speak effectively in front of audiences in the hundreds. Authored parts of presentations.
- **Sold speaking engagements** for athletes to large non-profit organizations, capturing 300% revenue increase.
- **Continued to attract and sign high-profile athletes despite downward industry trend** following key client's shift from external to internal sourcing for motivational speakers:
  – Targeted and booked athletes considered "unobtainable" by peers and supervisor.
- **Streamlined operations.** Implemented structure and categorized speakers (amateur/professional).

EARLY CAREER DEVELOPMENT

Susan Bergman, Producer and Composer, New York, NY
CO-PRODUCER
Coordinated production staff for *Hairspray, Into the Woods,* and *Jekyll & Hyde.* Managed fundraising and publicity.

- **Independently identified and capitalized on** market base expansion in Florida.

Green Apple Barter Services, New York, NY
ACCOUNT EXECUTIVE
Sold bartering memberships to private business owners in New York.

- **Doubled territory and business revenues in 6 to 8 months** by opening new market in Rockland County. Delivered sales training for peers to boost sales results.

Jill McNulty & Associates, New York, NY
CO-DIRECTOR OF ADVERTISING
Hired to research radio advertising and sell drive-time ads for major NY radio station.

- **Achieved substantial press coverage and exceeded expectations** by targeting persons and organizations previously not considered, successfully raising the bar.

EDUCATION

M.A. degree in Speech and Theater. Graduated with honors; 3.8 GPA.
B.A. degree in Speech, English, and Media Arts. Graduated with honors; 3.9 GPA.
BARUCH COLLEGE, New York, NY

Resume Transformation #2: Daniela R. Venise

Resume Writer:

Rosa E. Vargas, NCRW
Creating Prints Resume Writing Services
Phone: (407) 802-4962
E-mail: rvargas@creatingprints.com
www.creatingprints.com

The Situation

Daniela had enjoyed steady employment in the computer field for 25 years and had never had to actively look for a job—for each previous job change, she was recruited by someone who had worked with her before. Thus, when she was faced with a layoff due to a merger, she didn't have much experience or knowledge in writing a strong resume.

The "Before" Version

Daniela's "before" resume is a strict reverse-chronological summary that includes not even an Objective, never mind a Summary. It is filled with job descriptions and contains no indication of how good she was at her job. It includes no achievements.

The "After" Version—Applying the Five Resume Makeover Strategies

- **Fashion a Strong Framework.** This functional resume allows Daniela to present the totality of her experience and accomplishments in a consolidated fashion, and because the resume is just one page long, readers can quickly assess her education and career history as well as her accomplishments. In true functional style, her employment is listed at the bottom without descriptions or details.

- **Start with a Superlative Summary.** Notice the branding statement that appears just below Daniela's name. The entire heading—name, branding statement, and contact information—is bold and eye-catching. The Profile paragraph emphasizes both technical and non-technical capabilities, and the Technical Skills section creates a handy keyword summary of her core strengths.

- **Emphasize Experience and Accomplishments.** Daniela's key qualifying experiences are highlighted in a separate section that encompasses both capabilities and accomplishments.

- **Enhance with Education and "Extras."** Daniela's education is briefly and accurately stated; she does not have a degree but does have two years of very relevant education. Note, also, the Core Strengths section in the summary that mentions soft skills that will help to set her apart from other technical professionals.

- **Proofread and Polish to Perfection.** The design of Daniela's resume is a large part of its appeal. It took a good deal of editing and polishing to end up with an attractively formatted one-page resume.

Daniela R. Venise

3799 Millenia Blvd.
Orlando, FL 32839
Phone: 407-802-4962
drvenise@gmail.com

EXPERIENCE:

Office Automation, Orlando, FL (merger)   2002 to 2007
Analyst II
Support and maintain operations for the Mansfield Division. Troubleshoot network issues. Maintain
telecommunications, e-mail, Virus/Spyware removal and customer ordering systems. Helpdesk
Support for both in-house and customer needs, as well as on-site visits. PC and peripheral repairs and
installations.

Lan Communications, Orlando, FL (acquired Bresner)   1997 to 2002
PC/Lan Tech
Handled all PC installations and repairs. Upgraded hardware and software. User profile administrator.
Troubleshoot network issues. Convert all customers on OrderWriter ordering system to **ECHO.**
Helpdesk Support for customers ordering systems via phone, e-mail or onsite. Troubleshoot all in-
house users' technical issues.

Orlando Co., Orlando, FL   1989 to 1997
Operations Assistant
Maintained AS400. Organized backup procedures. Developed queries for reporting. Prepared and
Installed all new PCs. Customer support for all issues. Installed new **"OrderWriter"** ordering system
and HandHeld units and trained customers.

The Computer Company, Kissimmee, FL   1982 to 1989
Computer Operator
Control programmer's job flow and tape requests. Backed up all systems. Maintained all equipment.

ACHIEVEMENTS:
Removed outdated Windows PCs and introduced Windows 2000 and XP PCs. Installed equipment and
trained customers on latest ordering software. Programmed barcode readers and HandHeld units
(Symbol). Installed and configured wireless networks.

COMPUTER SKILLS:
Windows XP/2000/x, Windows Server 2000/2003, MS Office 2000/2003 (Word, Excel, PowerPoint),
MS Exchange, IBM iSeries (AS400), OS400, QUERY/400

REFERENCES:
Furnished Upon Request

Figure 4.3: Before.

Daniela R. Venise

▶ *Decreasing idle time and cementing customer loyalty by identifying and solving complex IT issues.*

drvenise@gmail.com
Tel: 407-802-4962

3799 Millenia Blvd.
Orlando, FL 32839

DESKTOP SUPPORT / FIELD IT TECHNICIAN

Troubleshooting ▶ Installing ▶ Repairing ▶ Upgrading ▶ Supporting

Profile: Instinctive problem-solver with more than 10 years of experience. Sharp PC maintenance technician with a combination of qualifications: wide-range technical knowledge, general business experience, and personable communication skills. Expert analyst with ability to investigate, identify, and solve complicated hardware, software, and operating system failures. Technician with exceptional ability to support end-users by reassuring them and by clarifying intricate technical information.

Technical Skills: Hardware, Software, and Peripherals Repair and Quality Assurance. Wireless Networks, Programming Scanners, User Profile Administration, Backup and Recovery, Reporting and Documenting. Troubleshooting, Field Support, Help Desk / User Support, Installation and Configuration.

Windows XP/2000, Windows Server 2000/2003, MS Office 2000/2003, IBM iSeries (AS400), OS400, and QUERY/400.

Core Strengths: Verbal Communications, Customer Service, and Interfacing with Upper Management

EXPERIENCE SUMMARY

- **Revamped computer systems:** Upgraded to Windows 2000, XP operating systems, and wireless networks.
- **Maintained, installed, and repaired complex IT issues:** Identified weaknesses, troubleshot network issues, maintained telecommunications, removed viruses and spyware, performed PC installations and repairs, upgraded hardware and software, and prevented systems failures.
- **Saved sensitive data:** Recovered data, backed up all systems, and kept all equipment functional on a 24-hour basis.
- **Converted computer phobics into competent users:** Provided instruction in a non-technical manner, training staff and customers via telephone, e-mail, and on site.
- **Helped companies recover and retain customers:** Developed excellent rapport with long-term customers. Answered e-mails promptly, addressed IT questions over the telephone, and guided customers, in person, through computer challenges.

EMPLOYMENT

IT Analyst / Support Technician, OFFICE AUTOMATION, Orlando, FL	2002–2007
PC Technician, LAN COMMUNICATIONS, Orlando, FL	1997–2002
Operations Assistant, ORLANDO CO., Orlando, FL	1989–1997

EDUCATION

University of Central Florida, Technical Degree Program, 2 years completed

Figure 4.4: After.

Resume Transformation #3: James Michael Bridges

Resume Writer:

Julianne Franke, MS, MRW, CPRW, CCMC
Breakthrough Connections
258 Shire Way
Lawrenceville, GA 30044
Phone: (770) 381-0876 or (404) 317-3316
E-mail: jfranke1@bellsouth.net

The Situation

James was looking for a higher-level sales job but had had no luck with a traditional chronological resume that included no quantifiable sales achievements.

The "Before" Version

James begins with a nice, clear objective, but the rest of his resume does not seem to support this goal. There are no achievements, and his two part-time positions while in college take up almost half the resume.

The "After" Version—Applying the Five Resume Makeover Strategies

- **Fashion a Strong Framework.** Keeping the chronological format, James's new resume paints the picture of a top sales performer. Functional subheadings are used within his two major positions to call attention to various areas of expertise while keeping the bullet points to a reasonable number.

- **Start with a Superlative Summary.** A clear headline and keyword subheading instantly communicate the key information for this job seeker. The profile paragraph is concise yet rich in the soft skills and character attributes that will distinguish him from other candidates.

- **Emphasize Experience and Accomplishments.** James's two most significant positions now make up the bulk of his resume. The accomplishments are full of specifics—numbers, percentages, and comparisons—that demonstrate his consistent top performance.

- **Enhance with Education and "Extras.** Notice how the keyword phrase "BS in Computer Information Technology" was appropriately worked into James's education section, even though he has not quite completed his degree. His two college jobs are briefly mentioned, along with the fact that he self-financed his education, because these facts demonstrate his work ethic. His Computer Technician job title is in bold because it supports his goal of a technology sales position.

- **Proofread and Polish to Perfection.** The resume's clean, professional appearance contributes to the picture of James as an accomplished sales performer.

James Michael Bridges
716 Georgetown Place Suite #2
Alpharetta, GA 30003
Home: 770-545-7676; Cell: 404-489-6666
jmbridges@gmail.com

Objective:
To obtain an entry to mid level sales position in a forward thinking, team oriented, technologically minded company.

Education:
3 years of Bachelor of Science in Computer Information Technology
Albany State College, Albany, Georgia
Focus: Computers, Sociology, and Psychology

Work Experience:
2004-Present *Mortgage Specialist,* American Mortgage Company, Atlanta, GA
- Originating mortgage loans in a high-volume shop.
- Training other mortgage specialists on products and sales techniques.

2003-2004 *Retail Location Manager,* Cingular Wireless, Alpharetta, GA
- Opening/Closing of the store with all keys and security codes.
- Sold AT&T Cellular Service, Phones, and Accessories.
- Utilized Cold-Calling for outside sales.
- Met With Media Salespeople to Develop Advertising Campaigns

2001-2003 *Vice President of Media,* The Richter Group, Charlotte, NC
- Developed and maintained relationships with over 100 small to medium sized corporations, facilitating working trade profit models.
- Worked with sales team to expand market share, locally on personal level and through national telemarketing programs.
- Brokered client travel itineraries on national scope and beyond.
- Designed and implemented media proposals for companies of various sizes and through varied mediums.

1996-1999 *Computer Technician,* Computer Information Services, Albany State College, Albany, GA
- Provided technical support in public computer labs and via telephone.
- Supported the school's computer network.
- Repaired and upgraded computers owned by the school.
- Learned and taught new software programs to students and staff.

1997-1998 *Community Advisor,* Grafton Hall, Albany State College, Albany, GA
- Facilitated positive community growth and safety in a first year student residence hall of 250 residents.
- Responsible for dispute arbitration, community event planning, and resource assistance.

References Available on request

Figure 4.5: Before.

JAMES MICHAEL BRIDGES

716 Georgetown Place Suite #2   Home: 770-545-7676
Alpharetta, GA 30003   **jmbridges@gmail.com**   Cell: 404-489-6666

SALES/MANAGEMENT PROFESSIONAL
Consultative Sales • Account Management • Sales Training & Team Building

Goal-oriented self-starter with proven success as a motivator and a team builder. Fast learner with rapid advancement based on demonstrated sales leadership and exceptional customer service. Strategic and proactive manager who consistently demonstrates excellent communication, relationship-building, and problem-solving skills. Record of integrity, dependability, and exceptional customer service.

PROFESSIONAL EXPERIENCE

AMERICAN MORTGAGE COMPANY, Mortgage Specialist/Account Executive, Atlanta, GA   2004–Present
(The nation's largest privately held home-equity lender, recognized for its entrepreneurial corporate culture. American achieved 370% growth from 2000 to 2003 with loan volume of $17.8 billion in 2003.)

Sales Performance & Operational Leadership

- Achieved ranking in top 10% of branch for a major lender promoting a broad range of conventional and non-conventional mortgage products using personalized consultative approach.
- Consistently generated 4 loans/month or $6000 in loan volume (twice the industry average).
- Brought in $8.8 million in first year with 4% profit per loan (average is 2½ to 3½ %).
- Exceeded $800,000/month in loan volume on several occasions, $300,000 above industry average (typically attained by top 2%). Wrote largest loan for the team to date.
- Managed entire loan process from origination to funding within 7 days (industry average is 30–45 days).

Sales Training & Team Building

- Interviewed, trained, and mentored new and existing Mortgage Specialists.
- Assumed leadership role as "go-to" person, team leader, and interim branch manager to sales team of 10–14.

CINGULAR WIRELESS, Retail Manager, Alpharetta, GA   2003–2004

- Increased sales 50% in the first 3 months, doubling previous quarter sales.
- Generated additional 10%–15% through cold calling, corporate repeat business, and marketing promotions.

THE RICHTER GROUP *(Promoted 5 times in 2 years)*, Charlotte, NC   2001–2003
Vice President of Media/Media Broker/Sales Rep/Travel Broker/Broker

Operational Leadership

- Established and maintained long-term referral relationships with major corporate accounts within the media industry as VP for an organized reciprocal trade organization with 280 members.
- Directed new branch office startup servicing the mid-Atlantic region; signed on 50 clients, 200% of target.

Sales Performance

- Prospected and brought on board 5–10 new accounts per month, exceeding quota of 1–2 clients per month. Achieved 100% client retention in a highly competitive industry.
- Doubled membership growth, leading to company expansion such that broker staff was increased by 150%.
- Negotiated trade for $100,000 in media planning within 3 weeks for a key account representing 70% of total company revenue, ensuring account loyalty and solidifying the firm's financial integrity.

EDUCATION/PROFESSIONAL CERTIFICATION

University of Phoenix, Business Administration, Major: Marketing (In progress)

Albany State College, Albany, GA (3 years of study toward BS in Computer Information Technology)
    Resident Advisor; employed 3 years as **Computer Technician;** self-financed 100% of tuition and expenses.

Licensed Loan Officer, Georgia, Louisiana, Florida, Tennessee (45 hours of training)

Figure 4.6: After.

Resume Transformation #4: Barbara Jenner

Resume Writer:

Carol Altomare, MRW, CPRW
World Class Resumes
Flemington, NJ 08822
Phone: (908) 237-1883
E-mail: wcr@worldclassresumes.com
www.worldclassresumes.com

The Situation

In the past Barbara had not needed a strong resume—she had been specifically sought out by her last two employers based on her excellent reputation and had excelled in demanding jobs that called on her strong skills in administration, customer relations, and project coordination. Recently, on a volunteer basis, she had become involved in fundraising for her nephew's special needs. She found out that not only did she excel at it, it awakened a passion in her to make a real difference in the world. She wanted her new resume to open doors in development or fundraising work but also be appropriate for business administration positions.

The "Before" Version

Barbara's "before" resume shows zero quantifiable achievements for her current position. In fact, this was her weakest experience and was in an industry—retail—that she wanted to get out of. Her earlier positions descriptions included lots of duties but no quantified achievements. Notice that she has relegated her unique "Strengths" paragraph to the end of the resume—a position that will probably be overlooked by employers who are underwhelmed with the first page.

The "After" Version—Applying the Five Resume Makeover Strategies

- **Fashion a Strong Framework.** A functional format allowed Barbara to bring together all of her relevant experience and accomplishments under headings that are rich in the right keywords for her current goals. Her contact information is placed at the bottom of each page; it is easy to find but doesn't detract from the overall page design.

- **Start with a Superlative Summary.** A headline and brand tagline position Barbara appropriately for her primary goal and can be easily changed for administrative positions she might apply for. Her profile paragraph mentions both hard and soft skills.

- **Emphasize Experience and Accomplishments.** Barbara's function section ("Select Accomplishments") is excellent because it includes specific, measurable achievements that are directly related to her goals. Notice that she identifies where each accomplishment took place—this will lower red flags and help employers understand her impact in each of her positions.

- **Enhance with Education and "Extras."** In Barbara's "before" version, her education looked scattered and incomplete, because she had attended several schools without graduating. The new version summarizes this educational background appropriately and concisely. Her "Extras" include computer skills and volunteer service—both entirely relevant to her objective.

- **Proofread and Polish to Perfection.** Barbara's accomplishments are carefully worded and were extensively edited to keep them crisp and to create the page break at an advantageous place—just following her three primary functional competencies. The added design elements surrounding her name and headings make this resume stand out.

Barbara Jenner
822 Meadow Drive
Mount Kisco, NY 10549

Phone: 914-666-8822
E: bjenner@aol.com

Professional Objective

Secure a management, sales, or administrative position that allows me to exercise my experience in negotiating, problem solving, purchasing and project management. The ideal position will allow me to highlight my skills with customer / client service.

Employment

Topps Appliance (5/2007-Present)
Three-store residential appliance retail chain

Store Assistant Manager
Position created for me to revamp store merchandising, manage sales team and drive retail sales.

Gilman Company (2005-4/2007)
Equipment dealer

Project Manager / Contract Estimator
- Recruited to this position for outstanding reputation and success at competing company.
- Formulated costing, and submitted bids on all new contracts.
- Negotiated costs with all vendors, from mfg. to carriers.
- Solely responsible for all customer service, and sales for all new and replacement equipment contracts.
- Researched new project opportunities.
- Chaired pitch-meetings and project planning / progress meetings.
- Documentation and administrative management of domestic and overseas correspondence, shipping and customs clearance.
- Functioned as office, database and contact manager.

Wentworth Equipment Company (2000-2004)
Equipment dealer

Project Manager
- Formulated cost, submitted bids, wrote and managed contracts for all new accounts.
- Negotiated costs with all vendors.
- Managed flow of project and information with all service providers, contractors, manufacturers, carriers, etc.
- Functioned as office manager.
- Additional duties included coordinating annual sales meeting, dinners and festivities for 500+ people, involving intricate travel schedules.

Figure 4.7: Before.

Barbara Jenner

822 Meadow Drive   Phone: 914-666-8822
Mount Kisco, NY 10549   E: bjenner@aol.com

EDUCATION:	Corning Community College RN Program: 1998-1999 Iona College BS Program: 1992-1993 Westchester County College Liberal Arts Program: 1992
STRENGTHS:	Powerful, effective relationship builder; this is my greatest strength. Strong, keen, savvy negotiator; this is what excites me most. Entrepreneurial spirit; I take pride and ownership of everything I do. Profound respect for budgets, expenses and opportunity costs.
COMPUTER LITERACY:	Hardware: PC Compatible and Local Networks Software: Windows XP, Microsoft Office suite (Outlook, Word, Excel), AutoQuotes

REFERENCES FURNISHED ON REQUEST

WILLING TO TRAVEL

❧ BARBARA JENNER ❧

FUND-RAISER / DEVELOPMENT ASSOCIATE
Dynamic professional with exceptional organizational skills and a flair for client relations

❧ **PROFILE** ❧

Well-regarded professional with excellent administrative skills and a proven record of success in customer-driven support roles. Capable program manager; a self-starter who is well equipped to manage and prioritize the competing demands of multiple projects. Proven relationship manager who is successful in establishing rapport and working with people at all levels. Respected team player known for bringing a sense of pride and ownership to all tasks and projects.

Core Competencies

- Project Management
- Program Coordination
- Relationship Building
- Problem Solving

- Event Planning
- Fund-raising
- Vendor Negotiations
- Client Management

❧ **SELECT ACCOMPLISHMENTS** ❧

Fund-raising/Event Planning

- Tapped to plan and coordinate large-scale meetings for 500+ contractors and sales reps, turned out three flawless events that were well received by attendees. Secured facilities, negotiated with vendors, and coordinated all administrative aspects to make each event a success. *(Wentworth Equipment)*

- Planned and executed all aspects of fund-raiser that attracted 430 attendees and raised $47,000 for the Brett Dayton Special Fund. Implemented communication plan and solicited donations from local residents and businesses, bringing in 170 auction and raffle items. Emceed event and hosted live auction.

Relationship Management

- Built reputation for customer-first approach in all positions held, developing strong customer relations that won contracts and promoted repeat business.

- Relied on to step in and resolve escalated customer issues as assistant manager, achieved considerable success in appeasing clients, going beyond the immediate issue to win client business long term. Saved $15,000 in potential lost sales with one customer alone. *(Topps Appliance)*

- Leveraged relationship management skills to save multimillion-dollar national account by agreeing to serve as sole contact for 30 individual locations across the US. *(Gilman Company)*

Project Management

- Managed purchase and installation contracts for two equipment dealers, handling everything from costing and bidding to scheduling and customer service. Managed projects ranging in size from $300,000 to $2 million. Successfully coordinated as many as five projects at a time. *(Gilman Company* and *Wentworth Equipment)*

- Applied project coordination and follow-up skills to win new contracts, including a national account that had previously refused to do business with company due to poor service. Won contract with Caesar's / Mt. Pocono through successful negotiation with third-party vendor to come in as low bidder. *(Gilman Company)*

822 MEADOW DRIVE ◆ MOUNT KISCO, NY 10549 ◆ (914) 666-8822 ◆ bjenner@aol.com

Figure 4.8: After.

Organizational Improvement

- Brought new energy to sales team, implementing one-on-one training to familiarize staff with automated computer systems and improve overall efficiency. *(Topps Appliance)*
- Developed new systems to manage flow of information on projects, improving office productivity. *(Gilman Company* and *Wentworth Equipment)*

❧ PROFESSIONAL EXPERIENCE ❧

TOPPS APPLIANCE   2007 to present
Assistant Manager
Recruited to fill specially created position, developing and implementing strategies to revamp operations, manage sales teams, and drive revenues.
- Established reputation for exceptional service, building loyal client base in high-end market.

GILMAN COMPANY   2005 to 2007
Project Manager / Contract Estimator
Recruited to position based on outstanding reputation. Formulated costs and submitted bids on all new contracts. Negotiated with vendors to get best pricing. Chaired pitch meetings and project planning / progress sessions. Provided general administrative support.

WENTWORTH EQUIPMENT COMPANY   2000 to 2004
Project Manager
Managed office while coordinating costing and bidding for purchase and installation projects. Negotiated costs with vendors. Planned and coordinated annual sales meeting.

❧ EDUCATION ❧

Completed more than 60 credits towards bachelor's degree.

❧ COMPUTER SKILLS ❧

Microsoft Office (Word, Excel, Outlook). AutoQuotes. Internet applications.

❧ VOLUNTEER SERVICE ❧

Fund-raiser / Event Coordinator for the Brett Dayton Special Fund.
Organized highly successful fund-raising event to raise funds for cancer research.

Resume Transformation #5: Paula Atkins

Resume Writer:

Georgia Adamson, MRW, CCM, CCMC, CPRW, CEIP, JCTC
A Successful Career, div. of Adept Business Services
1096 N. Central Ave.
San Jose, CA 95128
Phone: (408) 244-6401
E-mail: success@blueribbonresume.com
www.ablueribbonresume.com
www.asuccessfulcareer.com

The Situation

Paula's company was relocating to the East Coast, prompting her to update her resume and launch a job search for a local position.

The "Before" Version

Paula's existing resume focused heavily on job duties and did not make her strengths and expertise stand out. The format was uninspiring, and the document contained several typographical errors.

The "After" Version—Applying the Five Resume Makeover Strategies

- **Fashion a Strong Framework.** Paula's strong and relevant work history makes her a natural candidate for a hybrid/reverse-chronological resume.

- **Start with a Superlative Summary.** Paula's new summary is a masterful presentation of her capabilities and expertise. In just a few lines, it contains a strong profile paragraph, a keyword list, and some additional competencies in computer software and several foreign languages.

- **Emphasize Experience and Accomplishments.** Paula's resume writer was able to draw out from her several "success stories" that really shine on this resume. The position descriptions are quite brief, and the accomplishments are used to showcase not only her results but also the variety of business areas in which she was involved.

- **Enhance with Education and "Extras."** The before and after versions of Paula's resume are quite similar, with just a few extraneous details removed. As noted previously, her "Extras" are included in the Summary.

- **Proofread and Polish to Perfection.** Formatting enhancements are used to call attention to the headlines and to Paula's accomplishments. The result of careful editing and polishing is a well-written resume that presents a high-value candidate in a very attractive package.

Paula Atkins
2210 Stevens Road
Santa Cruz, CA 95060
(408)555-5555

CAREER OBJECTIVE: A management role in accounting department

QUALIFICATION HIGHLIGHTS:

- All around professional with successful experience and expertise in all phases of accounting and administration in manufacturing, service and retail companies.
- An efficient, accurate, hands-on managaer with excellent communication and leadership skills.
- Strong computer and analytical skills. Additional expertise with Great Plain, Peachtree, DacEasy, Windows, Word, Excel, Access and Lotus 1-2-3.
- Fluent in English, Chinese and Taiwanese

PROFESSIONAL EXPERIENCE:

Capture Technology, Soquel, California
Accounting Manager   *7/00-Present*

- Provide accurate and timely financial information to management. Prepare monthly and annually consolidated financial statements. Perform financial planning and analysis. Provide parent company (located in Sweden) with financial and management reports such as profit planning, cash forecast, budget and expenditure variance analysis.

- Improve accounting system: Set up and transfer accounting system using Peachtree. Develop accounting policies and procedures.

- Manage all aspects of accounting department: Manage AP, AR, General ledger, fixed assets, P&L, bank reconciliation, inventory control and monthly and year-end closing.

- Establish corporate tax accounts: Set up corporate tax account with several states. Prepare all government filings, reports and surveys.

- Coordinate semi-annual financial auditing: Be a primary contact and coordinate external CPA in audit processing. Assist CPA to file Federal and 14 States corporate income tax returns.

- Manage human resource and office administrative functions: Engage in establishing employee hand book. In charge of company payroll, retirement plan, insurance plan, and other employee's benefits. Participate in qualifying ISO 9001 standard.

Figure 4.9: Before.

Robinson Technology, Inc., San Jose, California
Sr. Accountant   8/96-7/00

- Manage full cycle of accounts payable: Effectively communicate with headquarters to recommend effective accounting measures to resolve price discrepancies. Issue check and make wire transfer payment. Carry out reimbursement of employee's expense reports.

- Perform accrual revenues and accounts receivable: Carry out timely AR collections, manage internal accounts, daily cash flow and perform monthly cash projections. Analyze and communicate with buyers for discrepancies, resolve payment and issue debit/credit memos for RMA returns. Perform accounts reconciliation in support of month end and year-end closing.

- Maintain monthly inventory reports and physical inventory counting: Consolidate inventory reports from consignment locations and perform monthly inventory reconciliation. Analyze inventory movements and effectively monitor consignment stock and ensure accurate inventory valuation.

Creative Electronics, Inc., Saratoga, California
Accountant   9/94-8/96

- Manage cash follow within company budget: Prepare bank reconciliation and analysis for daily credit card transactions, cash deposits and wire transfers.

- Perform month end close entries: Prepare recurring, general and adjustment entries. Reconcile AR and AP aging to resolve discrepancies. Perform regular Accounts Receivable and Accounts Payable daily duties. Search on lost or damaged merchandise by carrier and resolve UPS and FedEx claims.

- Coordinate with different department: Work with sales, purchasing and RMA departments on credit returns, price protection and incentives to ensure accuracy in billing.

- Maintain professional files: File all reseller's permits, invoices, purchase orders, cash deposit, vendor and customer agreements.

EDUCATION:
    Howard Business College, Des Moines, Iowa.
    Bachelor of Business Administration–Accounting 1994
    Outstanding Student Award, 1994
    Awarded Dean's List, 1/94. **Minor:** Computer Science

    Peking Technologies University, Peking, China
    Associate Degree of Mechanical Engineering 1984

REFERENCES: Available upon request

PAULA ATKINS

2210 Stevens Road, Santa Cruz, CA 95060   408-555-5555 • paula0001@yahoo.com

ACCOUNTING MANAGEMENT

Experienced Accounting Manager with a track record of delivering high-quality results and contributing to improvements that strengthen the bottom line of organizations. Experience spans multiple business environments, including companies in manufacturing, service, and retail industries.

Core Strengths & Expertise:

- Consolidated Financial Statements
- Financial Planning & Analysis
- Accounting System Setup
- Corporate Tax Accounts
- External Audit Coordination
- HR & Administrative Functions

Computer Software Competencies: Great Plains; Peachtree; DacEasy; MS Word, Excel, & Access

Languages: Multilingual—fluent in English, Chinese, and Taiwanese

PROFESSIONAL EXPERIENCE

Accounting Manager, **Capture Technology,** Soquel, CA   2000–Present

Manage all aspects of accounting for this Swedish-owned subsidiary, including accounts payable, accounts receivable, general ledger, fixed assets, bank reconciliation, inventory control, and monthly and year-end closings. Provide financial and management reports to the parent company. Manage Human Resources and administrative functions, including payroll and employee benefits, such as a retirement plan and health insurance. Supervise, train, and mentor a staff of 3 employees.

Accomplishment highlights:

- **Lowered insurance premiums approximately 15% with no reduction in coverage** by partnering with a broker to identify potential providers, compare fees and coverage, and obtain feedback from employees in 8 states. Selected a provider and plan that met all established criteria.
- **Improved the company's accounting system** by planning and completing a successful transition to Peachtree and by developing and implementing policies and procedures to ensure compliance with GASB standards.
- **Achieved a record of zero bad debt and no write-offs on $10 million–$30 million of revenue over a 7-year period.** Monitored A/R weekly, maintained close communication with the buyer, and initiated timely communications with customers to negotiate and resolve outstanding issues.
- **Passed all semi-annual audits and government sales tax audits without penalties.** Created and implemented an internal audit procedure, with assigned responsibilities for each team member. Conducted post-audit reviews to identify potential future improvements.
- **Completed payroll, corporate income, and sales tax filings correctly and on time for 15 states.** Acquired knowledge regarding each state's requirements and coordinated the tax process with the external CPA and the payroll service to ensure accurate and timely submissions.
- **Reduced office supply costs more than 30%** by establishing procedures to monitor and control both ordering and usage, including assignment of a specific employee to maintain responsibility.

Senior Accountant, **Robinson Technology, Inc.,** San Jose, CA   1996–2000

Performed a full range of accounting responsibilities, including A/P, A/R, collections, and inventory reporting and reconciliation. Key actions included the following:

- Communicated with headquarters to recommend effective accounting measures to resolve price discrepancies.

- continued -

Figure 4.10: After.

PROFESSIONAL EXPERIENCE
(continued)

- Managed timely A/R collections, internal accounts, daily cash flow, and development of monthly cash projections.
- Resolved payment questions and issued debit / credit memos for RMA returns.
- Maintained monthly inventory reports and physical inventory count. Consolidated reports from consignment locations and performed monthly reconciliation.
- Performed account reconciliation to support month-end and year-end closings.

Accountant, **Creative Electronics, Inc.,** Saratoga, CA   1994–1996

Performed diverse accounting responsibilities, including bank reconciliation; credit card transaction analysis; wire transfers; preparation of recurring, general, and adjustment entries; and reconciliation of A/R and A/P to resolve discrepancies. Collaborated with sales, purchasing, and RMA departments to ensure accurate billing on credit returns, price protection, and incentives. Searched for lost or damaged merchandise by carrier and resolved UPS and FedEx claims.

EDUCATION

Bachelor of Business Administration in Accounting, Minor in Computer Science
Howard Business College, Des Moines, IA, 1994
Dean's List; Outstanding Student Award

Associate Degree of Mechanical Engineering
Peking Technologies University, Peking, China, 1984

Resume Transformation #6: Jessica Jones

Resume Writer:

CJ Johnson, JCTC, CHRM, FJST, CCC, MSVA
Dream Coach®/ Military, Career & Transition Counselor/Certified Life Coach
Spirals of Success
P.O. Box 188
Sebastopol, CA 95473
Phone: (707) 396-3939
E-mail: cj@spiralsofsuccess.com

The Situation

While studying for the California bar exam, Jessica began her search for a legal position. She had recently completed law school, two internships, and a two-year stint as a law clerk.

The "Before" Version

Bland in appearance and filled with a combination of administrative and legal activities, Jessica's existing resume did not position her as a qualified attorney but rather a "glorified paralegal." The type was tiny and hard to read, there was no objective or summary, and her education was emphasized at the expense of her valuable work experience.

The "After" Version—Applying the Five Resume Makeover Strategies

- **Fashion a Strong Framework.** A hybrid/reverse-chronological format was selected as the best way to present Jessica's qualifications, particularly within the conservative legal profession. Her experience was bumped up to just below a new, strong summary, and her education—while important—took a more appropriate place at the bottom of the resume.

- **Start with a Superlative Summary.** Jessica's summary briefly summarizes her areas of legal experience—quite diverse for someone just out of law school, and also a great way to incorporate keywords into her resume. She also mentions her record of performance and her strongest skills areas. A bold headline makes her target crystal-clear.

- **Emphasize Experience and Accomplishments.** Rewritten to emphasize the value she contributed in each position, Jessica's experience and accomplishments now are the focal point of her resume. In her accomplishment statements she shows legal expertise, contributions to running a smooth and profitable law office, and leadership skills. A wonderful endorsement from her supervisor is framed in a gray box at the right.

- **Enhance with Education and "Extras."** A concise education section is enhanced by some "Extras" that include international study, language skills, and computer competencies.

- **Proofread and Polish to Perfection.** Presenting a clean, attractive appearance, the resume is highlighted by a few formatting enhancements, such as the gray box and the use of a different font for all the headlines.

JESSICA JONES
2000 Embarcadero Street
San Francisco, California 94114
(415) 544-2000
jesjones@yahoo.com

EDUCATION

Golden Gate University School of Law, San Francisco, CA
Doctor of Jurisprudence, May 2004
Activities: Completed 25 hours of Mediation Skills Training, Trial Advocacy

University of Oregon, Eugene, OR
Bachelor of Arts, May 2001
Major: **International Studies**   Minors: **Economics** and **Japanese**

Study Abroad: Tokyo International University, Kawagoe, Japan Fall 1999

Language Skills: Basic Japanese & Basic Spanish

Computer Competencies: PCs: Excel, Word, WordPerfect, Outlook, PowerPoint, Internet, Westlaw, LexisNexis, Summation, MPID, Timewriter, GroupWise

EXPERIENCE

Thomas, Ryan & Martin, LLP	Daly City, California
Law Clerk	2005-2007

- Law Clerk for fifty-attorney firm specializing in complex plaintiffs' asbestos litigation.
- 95% success rate on drafted motions, ex parte applications, and oppositions such as motions to compel, orders to show cause re: contempt, and motions for protective orders.
- Obtained valuable pre-trial information through drafted offensive discovery such as deposition notices, interrogatories, requests for admissions, requests for production of documents, and in-state and out-of-state subpoenas which resulted in earlier assessment of defendants' liabilities and more productive case management.
- Trained and helped supervise six incoming law clerks and six summer law clerks as needed.
- Hired and subsequently given two salary increases and year-end bonuses due to work accomplishments and commitment to the firm.
- In addition to preparing and submitting the above-finished documents to a supervising attorney for approval, I effectively corresponded with attorneys, clients, experts, court clerks, and third parties orally and in writing; maintained a calendar of assigned active cases and files; performed document reviews in various medias; and applied knowledge of court rules and procedures in preparing and filing documents in-state and out-of-state, including verifying citations and document formatting.

U.S. Department of Justice	San Francisco, California
Internship/Clinical Legal Education Program	Fall 2003

- Interned for a five-attorney office specializing in maritime litigation.
- Researched "maintenance and cure" issues, drafted memoranda, and helped with trial strategy.
- Assisted in preparation for depositions, reviewed complaints and pleadings, and other pre-trial discovery.

Stevens, Martin & Paulson, LLP	San Francisco, California
Internship/Clinical Legal Education Program	Spring 2003

- Interned for a ten-attorney office specializing in real estate litigation and construction law.
- Identified factual and legal issues through research, formulated relevant legal theories, and pursued strategies appropriate for the client concerning construction defects, warranties, and easements.
- Assisted with document review for a construction defect case.
- Effectively communicated with clients, opposing counsel, and the court through memoranda, letters, and briefs.

Figure 4.11: Before.

JESSICA JONES, J.D.
2000 Embarcadero Street, San Francisco, CA 94114
Home: (415) 544-2000   Cell: (707) 357-5377   E-mail: jesjones@yahoo.com

PROFESSIONAL LEGAL POSITION

Outstanding record of performance in planning, preparing, and managing high-profile cases. Expert analytical, investigative, organizational, negotiation, and litigation skills used to prepare powerful defense for construction defect, product liability, premise liability, tort liability, and other land use and management cases. Experience in asbestos, maritime, and real estate litigation.

Direct and decisive, with outstanding legal training and leadership and advocacy skills.

PROFESSIONAL EXPERIENCE

Law Clerk   2005–2007
Thomas, Ryan & Martin, LLP, Daly City, CA

Law Clerk for 50-attorney firm specializing in complex plaintiffs' personal injury including asbestos litigation, mold litigation, pharmaceutical, toxic tort, medical malpractice, automobile accidents, products liability, premises liability.

- Distinguished legal career highlighted by two salary increases and year-end bonuses for outstanding performance, astute legal skills, and strong ability to manage complex, sensitive matters.
- Achieved 95% success rate on drafted motions, ex parte applications, and oppositions; examples include motions to compel, orders showing cause regarding contempt, and motions for protective orders.
- Actively participated in the successful verdicts of product and premise liability cases resulting in the capture of a $19 million case and multiple multimillion-dollar cases.
- Successfully drafted offensive discovery containing deposition notices, interrogatories, requests for admissions, requests for production of documents, and in-state and out-of-state subpoenas. Obtained valuable pre-trial information resulting in early assessments of defendants' liabilities and more productive case management.
- Increased office productivity 50% by providing supervision and training for six incoming law clerks and six summer law clerks.

> *"Of all the Associates... by far the best skilled and most effective at offensive discovery."*

Internships
U.S. Department of Justice, San Francisco, CA *(Maritime litigation)*   2003
Stevens, Martin & Paulson, LLP, San Francisco, CA *(Real estate litigation and construction law)*   2003
- Researched "maintenance and cure" issues, drafted memoranda, and helped with trial strategy.
- Prepared depositions and reviewed complaints, pleadings, and other pre-trial discovery focusing on construction law, contract disputes, and corporate law.
- Identified factual and legal issues. Formulated relevant legal theories; researched and pursued appropriate strategies concerning construction defects, warranties, and easements. Assisted with document review for a construction defect case. Effectively communicated with clients, opposing counsel, and the court through memoranda, letters, and briefs.

EDUCATION

J.D., Golden Gate University School of Law, San Francisco, CA   2004
  • Trial Advocacy   • Mediation   • Litigation   • Contracts
B.A., University of Oregon, Eugene, OR   2001
  • International Studies   • Japanese   • Economics

ADDITIONAL EDUCATION AND SKILLS

Study Abroad: Tokyo International University, Kawagoe, Japan
Language Skills: Basic Japanese and Basic Spanish

Computer Competencies: Excel, Word, WordPerfect, Outlook, PowerPoint, Internet, Westlaw, LexisNexis, Summation, MPID, Timewriter, GroupWise

Figure 4.12: After.

Resume Transformation #7: Maria Rivera

Resume Writer:

Makini Theresa Harvey, CPRW, JCTC, CEIP, CCMC
Career Abundance
405 El Camino Real, #601
Menlo Park, CA 94025
Phone: (650) 630-7610
E-mail: makini@careerabundance.com

The Situation

Maria has a successful and extensive background as an Office Manager for dental offices. She wants to stay in that profession, but in a legal setting. However, law firms were not recognizing her ability to perform in a law office.

The "Before" Version

Maria's original resume is a chronological presentation of her career history. While her experience is relevant to her goal, the first thing that readers notice is that she is a "dental" administrator. Obviously this will not appeal to the law firms she is targeting. Also, her resume does not include any evidence of her effectiveness on the job.

The "After" Version—Applying the Five Resume Makeover Strategies

- **Fashion a Strong Framework.** A functional format allows Maria to showcase her accomplishments and de-emphasize the dental offices where she has worked.

- **Start with a Superlative Summary.** A bold headline and subheading that will appeal to her target audience are the new focal points of Maria's summary. She is quite clear about her objective to work in a law firm where her healthcare background will be of great value. Notice how the right keywords are used—words such as "practice manager" in the headline and an entire section of relevant core competencies.

- **Emphasize Experience and Accomplishments.** Functional headings on the left are balanced by strong experience and accomplishment statements on the right. Repeatedly, Maria shows how she has managed professional practices to benefit the firms and their clients.

- **Enhance with Education and "Extras."** Compare Maria's "before" education section with the "after" to see how certain items were pruned or edited because they placed her too squarely in the dental environment. Finally, the legal quote at the end of the page makes a strong statement for Maria's belief in the legal system. As a subtle finish, the three slashes that end the resume are the same marks that are used to fill space on pages of legal proceedings.

- **Proofread and Polish to Perfection.** Clean, crisp, and easy to read are the characteristics of this resume. Although quite possibly it could have been reformatted to fit on one page, the two-page format is highly strategic. It lets readers understand Maria's expertise before they see the environment in which she developed that expertise.

MARIA RIVERA
2922 Scott Avenue West
Denver, Colorado 80202
Cell: 303.768.4213
E-mail: mariarivera@aol.com

OBJECTIVE: To transition my extensive dental practice administrative skills into a law firm.

SKILLS SUMMARY:

- Organized and efficient with excellent planning and prioritization skills.
- Excellent oral and written communication skills.
- Effective project manager.
- Strong PC skills.
- Experienced in hiring, training and supervising other administrative and clerical personnel.
- Managed administrative operations for multi-site businesses.
- More than 15 years of experience managing dental offices.

EMPLOYMENT HISTORY:

RICHARD JONES, DDS, Denver, CO–2000 to Present
Office Administrator

The most senior-level administrative person in this large dental practice servicing more than 15,000 patients annually. Responsible for business policies and procedures, information technology, patient relations, billing and collections, general accounting, payroll processing, regulatory affairs, resources management, facilities management and insurance reimbursement. Managed 12-15 employees.

- Improved all administrative functions and systems, streamlined workflow, trained staff and improved patient relations.
- Introduced new PC-based systems to upgrade internal technologies and improve productivity.

KATHLEEN ALDEN, DDS, Denver, CO–1999 to 2000
Office Manager

Managed all accounting, administrative, patient relations, staffing, information technology, insurance and regulatory affairs for a small, private dental practice. Worked with software vendors to evaluate new practice management technology. Trained and supervised a staff of 4.

STEVEN HARVEY & ASSOCIATES, Littleton, CO–1997 to 1999
Office Administrator

Handled all administrative, billing, accounting, insurance reimbursement and patient relations functions. Managed a caseload of 5,000 patients each year and a staff of 2-4. Reduced employee turnover through improved training and motivational techniques.

Figure 4.13: Before.

MARIA RIVERA   Page Two
                              Cell: 303.768.4213
                         E-mail: mariarivera@aol.com

PINEVIEW DENTAL GROUP, Denver, CO–1995 to 1997
Practice Manager / Assistant Manager

Promoted from Assistant Manager to Practice Manager with the largest dental practice in the Denver metropolitan area. Practice served more than 35,000 patients annually. Hired, trained and supervised a staff of 15-20 administrative and clerical personnel.

RALPH WILKES & ASSOCIATES, Ames, CO 1993 to 1995
Practice Manager / Supervisor

Managed dental practice and supervised a staff of 6-8. Responsible for all practice management functions including patient relations, doctor scheduling, staffing, training, accounting, billing and collections, insurance reimbursement and a host of special projects.

THE DENTAL GROUP, Ames, CO–1992 to 1993
Office Manager

Managed 3 people and handled more than 3,000 patients each year. Responsible for all office management functions including greeting and assisting patients, answering phone calls, scheduling patients, filing insurance claims, managing accounts payable and accounts receivable, preparing monthly accounting reports and hiring and training new office staff. Assisted the doctors with personal matters as necessary.

EDUCATION:

Bachelor of Science Degree
Denver State University, Denver, CO, 2006

Certified Chiropractic Assistant, Denver College of Chiropractic, 1999

Continuing Education:

Effective Practice Management Techniques–Academy of Management Sciences
Patient Relations & Communications–Career Track
Effective Writing–Fred Pryor
Financial Management–Dun & Bradstreet
Insurance Billings & Collections–McVey & Associates
Introduction to PC Technology–Cerritos Community College
Patient Accounting–Dunbar Associates
Medical Office Management–Dunbar Associates

MARIA RIVERA

2922 Scott Avenue West
Denver, Colorado 80202

Cell: [303] 768-4213
mariarivera@aol.com

Professional Practice Manager
Committed to running an efficient, organized firm, driving profits, and exceeding client expectations

Enthusiastic and accomplished Office Manager seeking a position with a Personal Injury/Workers' Compensation law firm. Motivated team leader adept at improving client retention while boosting bottom-line performance.

- More than 15 years of successful experience turning failing offices into profitable practices.
- Excellent reputation for ethical performance, integrity, confidentiality/discretion, and client loyalty.
- Extensive knowledge and understanding of healthcare industry, legal aspects and regulatory affairs.
- Exceptional experience in overall practice operations, in large firms, boutiques, and multi-site businesses.

Core Competencies

§ Administration	§ Financial	§ People
▪ Business & Facilities Management	▪ Budget Administration	▪ Client Relations & Loyalty
▪ Legal & Regulatory Affairs	▪ Billings & Collections	▪ Confidentiality & Discretion
▪ Contract Negotiations	▪ Payroll Processing	▪ Human Resources
▪ Information Technology	▪ General Accounting	▪ Staff & Workflow Management

Selected Areas of Accomplishment

Practice Administration
- Exceeded all practice objectives for productivity, efficiency, quality, and performance.
- Reduced staff turnover through improved training and motivational techniques.
- Streamlined critical business processes and increased productivity and efficiency.
- Wrote employment ads, hired new staff, provided staff training, and facilitated performance evaluations.
- Supervised preparation of reports for insurance claims and legal and regulatory agencies.

Operations
- Exceeded collection goals. Reduced outstanding receivables by more than $100K by collecting judgments in small claims court.
- Worked closely with clients to collect outstanding debt.
- Prepared detailed financial reports, cost/benefit analyses, and other financial documents to improve practice management.

Client Loyalty
- Improved client retention through successful community outreach projects.
- Beat the competition through an innovative marketing program: Hired new hygienist and started early-morning appointments to accommodate clients. **Result:** Billings increased, covering hygienist's salary and other administrative costs within 6 months.
- Achieved record client gains for years 2000 through 2006, from 11,000 to 15,000–a 37% increase, while overhead costs grew only 25% in same period.
- Reduced client turnover from 17% annually to 8%.

Information Technology
- Spearheaded several PC upgrades and office automation projects. Successfully set up proprietary software systems and trained staff on those systems.
- Implemented state-of-the-art technology to improve productivity.
- Produced outstanding reports, proposals, presentations, marketing collateral, and more with effective use of Microsoft Office Suite programs.

Figure 4.14: After.

MARIA RIVERA   PAGE 2

─────────────────── Professional Chronology ───────────────────

Office Administrator, Richard Jones, Denver, CO   2000–Present
Office Manager, Kathleen Alden, DDS, Denver, CO   1999–2000
Office Administrator, Steven Harvey & Associates, Littleton, CO   1997–1999
Practice Manager / Assistant Manager, Pineview Dental Group, Denver, CO   1995–1997
Practice Manager / Supervisor, Ralph Wilkes & Associates, Ames, CO   1993–1995
Office Manager, The Dental Group, Ames, CO   1992–1993

─────────────────────────── Education ───────────────────────────

- BS Degree, Denver State University, Denver, CO, 2006
  -*Summa cum laude*

────────────────────── Professional Training ──────────────────────

- Effective Practice Management Techniques—Academy of Management Sciences
- Effective Writing—Fred Pryor
- Financial Management—Dun & Bradstreet
- Insurance Billings & Collections—McVey & Associates
- Introduction to PC Technology—Cerritos Community College

"Anyone who believes a better day dawns when lawyers are eliminated bears the burden of explaining who will take their place. Who will protect the poor, the injured, the victims of negligence, the victims of racial violence?"
—John J. Curtin, Jr., remarks to American Bar Association, Atlanta, 13 Aug. 1991, quoted in Time, *26 Aug. 1991, at 54*

/ / /

Resume Transformation #8: Felicia A. Garrison

Resume Writer:

Abby Locke, CARW, CPBS
Premier Writing Solutions, LLC
3289 Hardin Place NE
Washington, DC 20018
Phone: (202) 635-2197
E-mail: info@premierwriting.com
www.premierwriting.com

The Situation

While her core expertise was in marketing, Felicia had proven executive management strengths and wanted a position as a general manager or operations manager to utilize her wide scope of skills. She had spent the last 12 years in broadcasting and felt comfortable in that arena, although she was not limited to that industry.

The "Before" Version

Felicia's original resume was three full pages long, unfocused, and heavy on responsibilities and tasks with very limited attention to achievements and bottom-line impact. The bulleted format caused the responsibilities and limited achievements to blend together. The objective was focused on her interests rather than communicating her value to future employers.

The "After" Version—Applying the Five Resume Makeover Strategies

- **Fashion a Strong Framework.** Felicia's new resume is just two pages long but much more effective. It retains the chronological format but uses functional headings within each job to call attention to her areas of expertise.

- **Start with a Superlative Summary.** The new resume replaces Felicia's objective statement with a comprehensive summary that includes a headline, a powerful branding statement, a profile paragraph, and a keyword list. It presents "Felicia in a nutshell."

- **Emphasize Experience and Accomplishments.** Felicia's achievements are quantified and written in a tight style that makes the resume easy to skim. Notice the strong overall achievement statement at the beginning of each position description—it presents a capsule view of the value that she provided to each company. The bold and italic type set it apart.

- **Enhance with Education and "Extras."** Felicia has a classic educational background—BA in Marketing and MBA—that are perfect for her current goals. The Education section calls attention to these credentials in a very succinct format. Her MBA is also noted in the Summary.

- **Proofread and Polish to Perfection.** This is a great-looking resume that is easy to read. As noted, it took a lot of editing to create such crisp and high-impact achievement statements. The transformation of this resume proves the adage that "less is more"—two focused and polished pages are more meaningful and effective than the original three.

Felicia A. Garrison

8223 Parlane Drive
Falls Church, VA 22041
Phone: 202-658-2540 (C)
E-mail: fgarrison@hotmail.com

OBJECTIVE:
To become an integral part of established and challenging organization by utilizing my knowledge and management experience in the areas of International Business Development, Content Management, Business Administration, Marketing and Sales Strategies.

EDUCATION:
- B.A. (Marketing)
  University of Virginia, Charlottesville, Virginia, 1993
- MBA (Concentration in Marketing)
  Georgetown University, Washington, DC, 2005

CERTIFICATIONS AND LICENSES:
- Graphic Design & Multimedia Certification–CMI
- Computer Training–New Horizons

CAREER HIGHLIGHTS:

International World Television   **September 2001–Present**
Washington, DC
Regional Head of Sales for North America, Middle East, and Eastern Europe

International World Television, a subsidiary of France Telecom, specializes in DTH distribution of ethnic content over North America.

- Negotiated, developed and administered sales and marketing campaigns for the distribution of more than 110 ethnic television channels worldwide.

- Improved the concept of ethnic DTH distribution in North America via GlobeCast World Television with multiple services offering "Free-to-Air" and "Pay-TV."

- Implemented strategic planning, annual budgeting and cash flow-positive programs, subscriber's acquisition concept (SAC) and retention schemes.

- Enhanced customer service center, including developing telemarketing plans, caller campaigns, brochures and marketing letters, collateral, dealers' compensation plans, cross-promotion strategies and subscribers "Care" programs.

- Achieved more than $200 million in sales of satellite capacity over five years.

- Negotiated and won two U.S. government bids for services on Hispasat satellite for DTH distribution over Latin America and the Middle East.

- Top regional head of sales for the years of 2004, 2005 and 2006.

Figure 4.15: Before

- Expanded and launched 20 new Hot Bird television services over Europe with more than $15 million in new revenue.

- Negotiated and secured an agreement with LodgeNet for MDU and hotel / motel distribution which includes more than 6,000 hotel / motel outlets in North America.

- Instrumental in GlobeCast's World Television growth of services from 50 audio and video channels in 2001 to 200 by the end of 2006.

- Secured more than 60 major international contracts for distribution on IPTV platforms such as Verizon, Sivoo, MobiTV, and ConnecTV, in addition to distribution of G25 channels on Rogers Cable and Telus of Canada.

- Developed high-level business relations with broadcasting companies such as CNN, The Weather Channel, Encore Movie Channel, BBC World, The International Channel, Rogers Cable of Canada, Comcast Cable, LodgeNet, DD India, Asianet USA, RTV 21, RAI International, Trace TV, Fashion TV, ART, LBCI, Al-Jazeera TV, MediaZone, BroadRelay and many others.

International Television Corporation   **August 1995–September 2001**
Washington, DC
Director of Sales and Marketing; Corporate Liaison

Global Connections Television specializes in content distribution, production and marketing of international rights, especially from regions such as Europe and the Middle East.

- Developed and managed relationship between Global Connections Television and its affiliate channels with DISH Network / EchoStar Communications Corporation.

- Negotiated, administered and launched 7 new international video channels, and 4 audio International services on DISH Network satellites.

- Coordinated launch effort of new promotional sales and advertisement campaigns for ethnic and international consumers within specific marketing regions, metropolitan areas and rural U.S. domestic markets.

- Coordinated the migration of over 130,000 (Italian, Arabic) existing customers from 1 DISH Network satellite to another newer DISH Network satellite system in less than 9 months.

- Developed joint marketing and advertising programs to enhance domestic and International dealer network, distribution, operations and services for existing channels.

- Administered and trained Customer Service Representative (CSR), informative sessions at DISH Network outbound call centers, serving existing Italian, Arabic customers on the DISH Network DBS platform.

ABC International Marketing Division   **March 1992–August 1995**
Arlington, Virginia
Sales and Marketing Manager

Resume: Felicia Garrison   2

(continued)

(continued)

J.C. Penny's Direct Sales Division provides an easy and quick way to sell and purchase the hottest and newest commodity available in the USA.

- Performed Credit Netting; Demand Guarantee; Signature Guarantee; Irrevocable Letter of Credit; Sight Letter of Credit; International Trade; Bank Guarantee vs. Letter of Credit; Standby Letter of Credit; The World Trade Organization; Trade Finance.

- Performed implementation of policies and procedures, identifying current business issues, addressing corporate goals and objectives, strategic planning, budget overview and administration, directing other peers and subordinates, supporting top-level management, decision-making, and team building.

- Performed domestic and International sales and marketing strategic planning; developed marketing strategies, tracking market trends, negotiating contracts and agreements; developed domestic and international dealer networks and focused on advertising strategy.

- Excellent communication and proven interpersonal skill while working with others.

FOREIGN LANGUAGES:
Proficient in Arabic and English languages with superb familiarity with culture, religion and habits of most Middle Eastern and European countries.

COMPUTER PROFICIENCIES:
Proficient and possess the necessary skills in working with computers and Information technology tools including but not limited to Microsoft office bundles such as MS Word, Excel, Access, PowerPoint, most PCs, Window XP, ME, VISTA, NT and others.

Ability to work with ACT, Adobe Illustrator, Photoshop, PageMaker, Flash, and Subscriber Management System (CSG).

HOBBIES:
Skiing, racquetball, and swimming.

TRAVEL:
Japan, UAE, France, England, Lebanon, Jordan, Egypt, Kuwait, Saudi Arabia, Italy, Netherlands, Singapore, Philippines, Thailand, Israel, Bahrain, Qatar, Germany, India, Mexico, Canada, Serbia, Kosovo, Macedonia, Albania and many more.

ORGANIZATIONAL AND PROFESSIONAL MEMBERSHIPS:
- Member of the Arab American Marketing Association (AAMA)
- Member of the American Marketing Association-DC chapter
- Active member of the American Red Cross, Virginia Chapter
- Active member of the Animal Protection Association of Virginia

REFERENCES FURNISHED ON REQUEST

FELICIA A. GARRISON

8223 Parlane Drive, Falls Church, VA 22041
Cellular: 202-658-2540 ✦ E-mail: fgarrison@hotmail.com

SENIOR MANAGEMENT EXECUTIVE
Director / Senior Vice President / Vice President

"I deliver growth for companies—every time." Accurately forecasting industry trends and consumer interests that allow companies to exceed revenue projections, maximize ROI performance, achieve strong profitability, and realize significant market growth.

Accomplished, passionate senior executive with proven record of delivering unprecedented revenues, profits, and market performance for start-up, emerging, and growing companies operating in competitive, evolving industries. Forward-thinking strategist able to structure new program / service releases, finance investments, and joint ventures that increase business growth and minimize financial losses. Broad-based expertise with marketing to diverse cultural and ethnic groups in untapped, domestic, and international markets. MBA degree.

Core Marketing Management & Leadership Competencies

Strategic Market Planning & Direction	New Product / Program Development	Joint Ventures, Alliances, & Partnerships
Market, Industry, & Trend Analysis	Domestic & International Businesses	Revenue, Sales, & Profit Growth
Cross-Cultural Marketing Strategies	New Business Development	Corporate Branding Initiatives
Staff Recruitment & Leadership	Project Management & Execution	Customer Relationship Management

CAREER PROGRESSION

Regional Head of Sales—North America, Middle East, and Eastern Europe
International World Television, Washington, DC (2001 to Present)

Spearheaded company-wide initiatives that more than doubled revenues, tripled number of television channels, and strengthened company's position in the highly competitive broadcasting industry.

Scope: Implement innovative marketing strategies, advertising campaigns, and dealer incentives that spur business growth and service expansion. Oversee development of telemarketing plans, marketing brochures and letters, and cross-promotional programs. Collaborate closely with senior management to initiate programs and services that support long-term business growth objectives.

▸ **Business Growth:** Drove new operational, marketing, and business development strategies that impacted significant revenue growth from $18 million to $40 million.

▸ **Sales & Revenue Expansion:** Generated more than $200 million in annual sales over five-year period through new satellite capabilities.

  – Earned company reputation for achieving highest sales number in 2004, 2005, and 2006. Consistently increased sales by 25% each year.

▸ **New Program Development:** Played a pivotal role in influencing senior management to introduce Pay TV capabilities that helped company expand from 50 to 250 television channels.

  – Initiated 20 new "hot-bird" television services in Europe and achieved $15 million in new revenues for five consecutive years.

▸ **Contract Negotiations & Agreements:** Negotiated and acquired lucrative agreement with LodgeNet, the largest company in the hospitality industry, and increased channel / service distribution to more than 6,000 motel / hotel outlets in North America.

  – Generated $10 million in new revenues by consulting and settling on two U.S. government bids (for Hispasat satellite services) for DTH distribution in Latin America and the Middle East.

  – Landed 60 international IPTV contracts with major companies (Verizon, AT&T, MobiTV, ConnecTV) for additional channel distribution.

▸ **New Business Development:** Forged high-level business relationships with broadcasting companies that included CNN, The Weather Channel, Encore Movie Channel, BBC World, The International Channel, Rogers Cable of Canada, and Comcast Cable.

Figure 4.16: After.   *(continued)*

(continued)

FELICIA A. GARRISON   PAGE TWO

Director of Sales & Marketing / Corporate Liaison
International Television Corporation, Washington, DC (1995 to 2001)

Launched aggressive sales strategy that propelled company growth from start-up phase to $10 million in annual revenues despite mounting industry competition and high-level financial risk.

Scope: Recruited by president to join new company that recently acquired the rights to two television channels. Assumed directive to grow business operations; lead marketing, promotional, and advertising campaigns targeted at ethnic and international customers; and build corporate brand. Managed vendor, dealer, and affiliate relations.

- **Business Growth:** Launched aggressive channel distribution, customer acquisition, and marketing strategies that attracted 200,000 new customers in record time.
- **Staff Training & Development:** Orchestrated comprehensive training and supervision of more than 300 customer service representatives serving a multi-cultural, multi-ethnic customer base.
  - Provided direction on wide scope of customer relations techniques addressing cultural differences, ethnic nuances, and customer opposition.
- **Marketing Direction & Planning:** Instituted standard procedures for marketing campaigns, employee operations, and dealer incentive programs.
- **Executive Advisement:** Partnered with vice president of sales and marketing and president to conceptualize sales, marketing, and business growth strategies.
- **Project Planning & Leadership:** Steered comprehensive project involving conversion of 130,000 international customers, supervision of 12 employees, and development of new marketing campaigns. Completed project in nine months versus anticipated 12- to 18-month timeline.

Sales & Marketing Manager
ABC International Marketing Division, Arlington, VA (1992 to 1995)

Exceeded sales and revenue projections by devising structured campaigns and leading strategic planning efforts for global sales in un-penetrated markets.

Scope: Directed myriad activities impacting new policies and procedures, new business opportunities, corporate goals and objectives, domestic / international dealer networks, contract negotiations, advertising, and budget administration. Reported to director of sales and marketing.

- **International Business:** Instituted new financial documents, business contracts, and letters of agreement that allowed company to conduct business internationally.

EDUCATION

MBA in Marketing, Georgetown University, Washington, DC (2005)
BA in Marketing, University of Virginia, Charlottesville, VA (1993)

Resume Transformation #9: Robert Smiley

Resume Writer:

Louise Kursmark, MRW, CPRW, JCTC, CEIP, CCM
Best Impression Career Services, Inc.
24 White Oaks Lane
Reading, MA 01867
Phone: (781) 944-2471
E-mail: LK@yourbestimpression.com
www.yourbestimpression.com
www.resumewritingacademy.com

The Situation

After a stint in the military, Robert had moved to the financial services industry and had rapidly risen to the position of Vice President at a major Wall Street firm. He was then recruited to sales leadership roles with two smaller firms and subsequently joined a software company that sold products to the financial industry. In his three more recent positions, Robert felt he had not been that successful and therefore didn't know how to present the information on his resume.

The "Before" Version

Robert's initial resume starts with a Summary that emphasizes his leadership skills but doesn't clearly communicate who he is. His experience section is overloaded with job activities and short on accomplishments. His military section seems rather detailed given its age and the fact that he is not pursuing a career in the military or aviation fields. In a brief "Personal" section Robert communicated his passion for mountain-climbing and strenuous athletics.

The "After" Version—Applying the Five Resume Makeover Strategies

- **Fashion a Strong Framework.** Still two pages in length and still employing a chronological format, Robert's new resume follows a similar framework to his original version. However, the design is strikingly different.

- **Start with a Superlative Summary.** Beginning with a headline that clearly communicates who Robert is—a senior executive with expertise in two related industries—the Summary continues with two strong profile paragraphs that convey both his leadership strengths and his specific functional expertise. The most striking part of the Summary is Robert's branding statement, which translates his interest in mountain climbing into personal attributes that explain how he does what he does.

- **Emphasize Experience and Accomplishments.** Although Robert believed that his current and most recent positions had been less than successful, through introspection and consultation he was able to come up with a number of strong achievements and to quantify at least a few of them. Most notably, his current position now appears to be a responsible and significant role. A strong "wow" achievement introduces each position description. Robert's military background is still included but is much less prominent.

- **Enhance with Education and "Extras."** Robert attended two name-brand schools, the US Naval Academy and the Wharton School, that are highlighted in his Education section. His Wharton MBA is also noted in the Summary. The "Personal" section has been retained and just slightly condensed. It serves as a supporting "footnote" to the branding statement that opens the resume.

- **Proofread and Polish to Perfection.** A more elegant font and gray-shaded boxes enhance the appearance of Robert's resume.

Robert Smiley

17 Mohawk Trail, Chappaqua, NY 10514
914-555-1234
rsmiley@optonline.net

PERSONAL SUMMARY

Proven, dynamic leader with over twenty years of experience in a myriad of challenging positions. Hands-on expertise includes project planning and management, business development, risk management, marketing and sales support, along with full P&L responsibility. Skilled collaborator with proven success managing diverse teams. Passionate believer in setting clear goals and priorities along with moving projects to completion—skillful in the art of getting things done. A high-energy leader with very strong people skills.

PROFESSIONAL EXPERIENCE

FINCH FINANCIAL SYSTEMS, INC., New York, NY   September 2000–Present
New Products Group, Research and Development
- Responsible for strategic direction of capital markets project development.
- Actively involved in North America region sales support effort for Fixed Income, Interest Rate and Credit Derivatives products.
- Successfully implemented and completed three-year fixed-income front-office development project—this project "broke the mold" in terms of innovation, flexibility and functionality.
- Member of firm-wide Staff Development Committee—support and implement various leadership initiatives.

SMITH, SMITH & BARNES, INC., New York, NY   May 1998–January 2000
Vice President, Proprietary Trading Desk
- Senior proprietary fixed income trader in U.S. capital markets.
- Member of Firm Risk Committee—established new processes for the implementation of firm-wide risk controls.
- Developed firm-wide quantitative models for trading and sales desk—this included fitted curve analysis, statistical and graphical analysis of trade ideas and advanced relative value models.

GROVER SECURITIES, INC., New York, NY   June 1995–May 1998
Vice President, Government Securities
- Led the STRIPS and proprietary trading effort for USD trading desk—achieved excellent proprietary trading results using newly developed interest rate trading methodologies.
- Successfully implemented advanced risk-measuring techniques to better measure duration and yield curve risk for specific trades and the overall portfolio—this included using statistical methods to measure synthetic duration risk of individual treasury issues along with the implied curve and duration risk of basis and STRIPS trades.

Figure 4.17: Before.   *(continued)*

(continued)

MERRILL LYNCH & COMPANY, INC., New York, NY   July 1990–May 1995
Vice President, U.S. Government Trading
- Co-head and head of STRIPS trading desk. Generated and maintained superior profitability ($200 million trading profits) for the desk over a five-year span.
- Implemented new metrics for measuring and managing risk levels for one of the largest positions in the Fixed Income Division worldwide. This risk included, but was not limited to, duration risk, yield curve risk, curvature risk, basis risk and volatility risk.
- Actively managed new business development for the STRIPS business, including daily trading and flows, customer trade ideas and initiating new client relationships.
- Developed relative value tools, models and databases to analyze the yield curve for both STRIPS and coupon bonds. This proprietary information was used to better assess the risk/reward of both new trade ideas and existing positions.

UNITED STATES MARINE CORPS
Captain, Naval Aviator   May 1984–May 1990

- Spent six years undergoing intense training as a Marine Corps officer in highly stressful and diverse environments.
- Graduated from Naval Flight School as Marine Corps pilot—commanded flight missions throughout the United States and Asia.
- Recognized by Commanding Officer as top performing junior officer in the squadron two years running.
- Achieved increasingly responsible positions during six years as a Marine Corps officer.

EDUCATION

THE WHARTON SCHOOL, University of Pennsylvania   Philadelphia, PA
Master of Business Administration, May 1992

UNITED STATES NAVAL ACADEMY   Annapolis, MD
Bachelor of Science in Naval Architecture, May 1984

PERSONAL

Experienced marathon runner—completed three New York Marathons
Avid climber and mountaineer—successfully climbed Mt. Rainier, Mt. Whitney and other high points

ROBERT SMILEY

914-555-1234   17 Mohawk Trail, Chappaqua, NY 10514   rsmiley@optonline.net

SENIOR EXECUTIVE: FINANCIAL SERVICES/IT SERVICES

Continuously setting "Mount Everest" goals and pursuing those goals
with passion, energy, focus, and determination.

Strategically focused leader with repeated success introducing new concepts, building support for innovative ideas, motivating people to excel, and executing key initiatives across complex enterprises. In diverse positions throughout career—from U.S. Marines aviation officer to Wall Street trader to software company executive—consistently rose to new challenges and excelled in fast-paced, high-risk environments.

Accomplished marketing/business development/operations executive with deep knowledge of financial services, financial systems, and the complexities of global financial trading. Expert in designing and implementing best-in-class structures, processes, and methodologies as the foundation for consistent operations and continuous growth. Wharton MBA.

EXPERIENCE AND ACHIEVEMENTS

FINCH FINANCIAL SYSTEMS, INC.   New York, NY, 2000–Present

Marketing/Business Development/Product R&D Executive

Spearheaded strategic business initiatives to fuel growth, strengthen internal capabilities, and propel market expansion of privately held company that provides transaction solutions to the world's largest financial institutions. Assume multiple roles and diverse leadership responsibilities within fluidly structured technology firm—initiate, gain executive support, and lead complex initiatives across the organization.

- Identified major shortcomings in software design and drove a critical 3-year project to develop new solution that "broke the mold" in terms of innovation, flexibility, and functionality. Implemented project management controls, clearly defined milestones, and harnessed resources across the organization. New software became the centerpiece for sales efforts.
- Driving force behind company adoption of Core Business Values. Conceived idea and gained support of CEO to drive formal adoption of values that serve as guideposts for company programs, policies, and behaviors.
- Defined a sweeping new approach to software development/software quality.
- Added value to sales efforts through deep expertise in marketing, selling, and presenting to financial entities. Became integral part of pre-sales preparation for Fixed Income, Interest Rate, and Credit Derivatives products.
- Accelerated business development into the capital markets arena, paving the way for $7M in new business.
- Led key initiatives to build business capability and develop leaders as a member of the firm-wide Staff Development Committee.

SMITH, SMITH & BARNES, INC.   New York, NY, 1998–2000

Vice President, Proprietary Trading Desk

Recruited to senior trading role for proprietary fixed-income in U.S. capital markets. Strengthened processes, controls, and methodologies firm-wide.

- Introduced the first formal tools for trading and sales desk to quickly assess risk—quantitative models, statistical analyses, and graphs that fostered consistent and easy-to-use methodology. Made tools available to entire trading/sales team.
- As a member of the Firm Risk Committee, established new processes for implementing risk controls firm-wide.

Figure 4.18: After.   *(continued)*

(continued)

ROBERT SMILEY

914-555-1234   Page 2   rsmiley@optonline.net

GROVER SECURITIES, INC.   New York, NY, 1995–1998

Vice President, Government Securities

Brought on board to head **STRIPS and proprietary trading**—part of a strategic corporate initiative to strengthen the company's trading performance. Drove the development and adoption of new techniques and methodologies to create a strong foundation for the expanding trading operation. Managed trading and administrative team.

- Independently generated $3M+ trading profits each year, performing in the top tier of traders at the firm.
- Introduced advanced measurement techniques to better evaluate risks for specific trades and overall portfolio.

MERRILL LYNCH & CO., INC.   New York, NY, 1990–1995

Vice President, U.S. Government Trading, 1992–1995

Generated and maintained superior profitability ($200M trading profits) for the STRIPS trading desk over a 5-year period. Tapped to fill interim leadership role, hit the ground running and converted interim assignment to VP promotion. Actively managed new business development, including overseeing daily trading and flows, implementing customer trade ideas, and initiating new client relationships. Managed staff of junior traders.

- Grew profitability nearly 3-fold in 5 years.
- Honed decision-making skills daily in fast-paced, high-risk trading environment.
- Implemented new metrics for measuring and managing risk levels for one of the largest positions in the Fixed Income Division worldwide.
- Developed relative value tools, models, and databases to analyze the yield curve and better evaluate risk/reward of new ideas and existing trade positions.
- Led the Wharton recruiting effort for the Fixed Income Division from 1993–1995.

Bond Trader, 1990–1992

U.S. MARINE CORPS   1984–1990

Captain/Naval Aviator

Completed intensive training in a high-stress environment; commanded flight missions throughout U.S. and Asia. Top-performing junior officer in the squadron 2 years running.

EDUCATION

THE WHARTON SCHOOL, University of Pennsylvania   Philadelphia, PA, 1992
MBA, Major in Finance

UNITED STATES NAVAL ACADEMY   Annapolis, MD, 1984
BS, Naval Architecture

PERSONAL

Completed 3 New York Marathons.
Climbed Mt. Rainier, Mt. Whitney, and other peaks.

Resume Transformation #10: Beth Larson

Resume Writer:

Marjorie Sussman, MRW, CPRW
411 Washington Ave.
Cliffside Park, NJ 07010
Phone: (201) 942-8237
E-mail: marjorie1130@aol.com

The Situation

Beth had just graduated from college and was looking for summer and part-time work while she attended grad school. She didn't have a particular job in mind and needed a resume that gave an overview of her capabilities.

The "Before" Version

In this typical new-grad resume, nothing stands out and there is no indication as to the individual's skills and capabilities. It is difficult to determine what kind of job she is seeking and how she can help an organization.

The "After" Version—Applying the Five Resume Makeover Strategies

- **Fashion a Strong Framework.** The "after" version of this resume retains the chronological format and puts education up front as one of this new grad's strongest qualifications.

- **Start with a Superlative Summary.** A new summary in the "after" version clearly communicates Beth's skills and capabilities. It does not try to make her something she is not, but it enables readers to visualize where she might fit into their organization.

- **Emphasize Experience and Accomplishments.** A good description of job activities provides further evidence of Beth's skills.

- **Enhance with Education and "Extras."** Only the most impressive of Beth's college "extras" are included, and they are positioned within the Education section instead of their own section.

- **Proofread and Polish to Perfection.** A new format adds "pizzazz" to Beth's resume. Notice how things as simple as a different font for her name and a vertical line at the margin create a distinctive document.

Beth M. Larson

Home Address: 310 Pine Street, Crandall, NJ 07070
School Address: 24 Small Street, West Lafayette, IN 47933
E-mail Address: blarson@purdue.edu
Phone: (317) 666-6690

Education:

Purdue University, West Lafayette, IN   January 2005- December 2008
  Bachelor of Arts in Anthropology, Minor in Communications
  GPA: 3.4/4.0
Southern Methodist University, Dallas, TX   August 2004- December 2004
  General Studies
Seton Hall University   Spring 2009
  Beginning Master's Degree in Museum Studies

Work Experience:

Secretary to Principal   June 2008- August 2008
Yardley Public School, Yardley, NJ
      Organized and completed multiple projects for current student records
      Completed various receptionist duties related to computer work and phone work
      Performed tasks needed to complete purchasing orders for school
Assistant/Volunteer to Interim Executive Director   May 2008- June 2008
Tippecanoe County Historical Museum, Lafayette, IN
      Helped organize collections
      Researched items for accurate information and origins
      Organized visitors information and documented data obtained from studies
      Assisted with non-profit brochures and public communication to spread awareness
Editorial Assistant   June 2007- August 2007
Metropolitan Corporate Counsel, Mountainside, NJ
      Demonstrated good organizational and time management skills
      Performed above expected level- received 50% raise after 2 weeks
      Documented interviews used for articles in publication
      Organized and maintained membership database
Receptionist   May 2005- August 2005
Southern Exposure Tanning, Indianapolis, IN
      Developed positive customer relations
      Quickly acquired responsibilities of opening and closing store
Legal Secretary   June 2000- August 2004
Monument Title, Yardley, NJ
      Completed numerous legal forms and documents for real estate closings
      Communicated with other attorneys to coordinate and complete closing of title
      Excelled in computer literacy

Affiliations and Honors:

    - Deans List
    - Academic Honors Society
    - Delta Gamma Sorority member, House Art Director ('06-'07)
    - Anchor Splash philanthropy worker (raises money for the blind)
    - Museum Volunteer
    - Anthropology Club
    - Intramural Sports: Soccer, Indoor Soccer, Flag Football

Figure 4.19: Before.

Beth M. Larson

317-666-6690 ~ blarson@purdue.edu

Mailing: 24 Small Street ~ West Lafayette, Indiana 47933
Local: 310 Pine Street ~ Crandall, New Jersey 07070

QUALIFICATIONS

Highly motivated, upbeat Purdue graduate (5/2008) experienced in administrative support, customer service, and front-desk reception. Quick learner, committed to top-quality job performance. Dependable and courteous with superior communication and interpersonal skills. Excellent time management and organizational abilities. Proficient in Internet research, editing, proofreading, data entry, and transcription. Computer skills include MS Word, PowerPoint, Paint, Outlook, and Excel (basic).

EDUCATION

Bachelor of Arts in Anthropology, PURDUE UNIVERSITY, 5/2008
~ Dean's List, Academic Honors Society, Anthropology Club, Tippecanoe Museum Volunteer, Delta Gamma Sorority House Art Director, Volunteer Fundraiser (raised $10,000 for the blind)
Candidate, Master of Arts in Museum Studies, SETON HALL UNIVERSITY, start spring 2009

WORK EXPERIENCE

Secretary to the Principal
YARDLEY PUBLIC SCHOOL, Yardley, NJ   Summer 2008
✓ Supported the Principal, Superintendent, Head of Purchasing, and Child Study Team.
✓ Screened and routed phone calls, took messages, responded to e-mails, organized filing system.
✓ Updated student records, created student forms, prepared information packets for parents.
✓ Processed supply ordering: obtained approvals, verified sources of funding, confirmed deliveries.

Assistant to the Interim Executive Director
TIPPECANOE COUNTY HISTORICAL MUSEUM, Lafayette, IN   Spring 2008
✓ Organized and researched the origins of collections, ensuring accuracy of descriptions and corresponding reference numbers.
✓ Assisted in creation of brochures and direct-mail communications promoting the museum, raising funds, and soliciting memberships.

Editorial Assistant
METROPOLITAN CORPORATE COUNSEL, Mountainside, NJ   Summer 2007
✓ Provided editorial and research assistance to publisher of monthly law journal.
✓ Organized and updated membership database.
✓ Assisted advertising manager in ad creation and website updates.
✓ Transcribed content of phone interviews for inclusion in publication.

Manager/Receptionist
SOUTHERN EXPOSURE TANNING, Indianapolis, IN   Summer 2005
✓ Managed daily operations: opening and closing store, money handling, and customer service.

Legal Secretary
MONUMENT TITLE, Yardley, NJ   Summers 2000–2004
✓ Maintained high degree of accuracy in processing real estate legal forms and documentation.
✓ Interfaced with outside attorneys to coordinate and complete title closings.
✓ Provided full range of secretarial support.

Figure 4.20: After.

Resume Transformation #11: Ronald Woolworth

Resume Writer:

Marjorie Sussman, MRW, CPRW
411 Washington Ave.
Cliffside Park, NJ 07010
Phone: (201) 942-8237
E-mail: marjorie1130@aol.com

The Situation

Ron was seeking a very specific sales/business development position within the Media and Entertainment practice at IBM. He had great experience—a combination of technical sales and sports/media/entertainment sales and marketing. His "before" resume, however, is text-heavy and long at three pages, and it's not easy to see what he has accomplished.

The "After" Version—Applying the Five Resume Makeover Strategies

- **Fashion a Strong Framework.** A classic reverse-chronological format makes the most sense for Ron, who has progressive career experience and name-brand employers.

- **Start with a Superlative Summary.** Although Ron's original Objective is clear, it is not really necessary and it limits his resume to that one position. So the "after" version eliminates the Objective and employs a more effective headline. Instead of a vague "Experienced Business Professional," the headline proclaims his specific expertise in business development within the industry segments he is targeting.

- **Emphasize Experience and Accomplishments.** Bold type is used to draw attention to Ron's stellar sales and business development achievements, and position descriptions are limited to essential information to promote a quick read.

- **Enhance with Education and "Extras."** Ron's "affiliations" section is a strong addition to his qualifications, while his education is presented neatly and concisely.

- **Proofread and Polish to Perfection.** Ron's new format makes efficient use of space, reducing his resume from three pages to two and creating a more professional image.

RONALD B. WOOLWORTH
4545 LITTLETON RIDGE
ATLANTA, GEORGIA 30355
(555) 552-5534
RONALDBWOOLWORTH@YAHOO.COM

EXPERIENCED BUSINESS PROFESSIONAL

OBJECTIVE
Secure the Business Solution Professional position in IBM's Media and Entertainment Practice.

SUMMARY
Fourteen years of sales, entrepreneurship, business development, consulting, and leadership experience in entertainment, technology, and media industries. A talented innovative, tenacious, resilient, focus and ambitious, professional with demonstrated communication, interpersonal, strategic, analytical and technical skills that were cultivated as an entrepreneur, sales specialist, territory sales manager, account executive and accounting major. Particularly astute at working with groups in challenging environments as well active in headship and advisory roles in various professional and community organizations.

PROFESSIONAL JOURNEY

HEWLETT PACKARD COMPANY/TECHNOLOGY SOLUTIONS GROUP/MAY2006-PRESENT
INDUSTRY STANDARD SERVER SALES SPECIALIST

- *Led and partnered* with HP account teams to identify, develop, qualify and close HP BladeSystems business in assigned accounts and territory. *Created* and executed detailed sales plan to achieve revenue objectives. *Maintained* monthly forecast and sales pipeline. *Developed and preserved* close working relationships with appropriate internal and external BladeSystem resources and partners.
- *Participated* in account planning and strategy activity. *Leveraged* BladeSystem sales and support resources. *Presented* Industry Standard Server (ISS) BladeSystem benefits, features and value differentiation to improve HP's win rate with BladeSystem based solutions. *Articulated* appropriately at all customers levels the ISS BladeSystem roadmap for products features and benefits
- *Increased* awareness and interest in HP BladeSystem solutions in assigned territory or accounts Sustained high level of knowledge on HP BladeSystem products, roadmaps, competition, pricing, market share, and key BladeSystem differentiation. Identified business opportunities in account and territory base.

Figure 4.21: Before.　　　　　　　　　　　　　　　　　　　　*(continued)*

(continued)

FAN-O-MANIAC MEDIA GROUP/MARCH 2004-2006
CONSULTANT
- *"Played"* a key role in transitioning the concept into a media solution for clients
- *"Spearheaded"* the execution of the Fan-O-Maniac pilot:
  - Identify key media talent in the marketplace for the shooting of the pilot
- *"Leveraged"* salient relationship to secure meetings with C-level executives in the local broadcasting and sports industries
- *"Organized"* and recommended the internal professional team to deliver the concept to key external decision makers
- *"Crafted"* and *"researched"* the marketing proposal that was presented to clients.

MARKETSOURCE/HEWLETT-RETAIL   PROGRAM/OCTOBER   2001-FEBRUARY 2004
TERRITORY SALES MANAGER

- Responsibilities were :
  - Market Identification/penetration of new products, Customer management and satisfaction
  - Team leadership and motivation, expert product knowledge, new product, service launch
  - Product positioning, presentations, demonstrations/lunch and learns
  - Train new hires and competitor analysis

Managed, hired, and educated a part-time sales professional staff of five. Communicate competitive intelligence on thirteen retail product categories from Hewlett-Packard to retail sales representatives from Best Buy, Comp USA, Office Max, Office Depot, and MicroCenter. Created and executed marketing and promotional objectives from our national and regional offices.
  - 1st place for the "Bring it Home Tour" Best Recap and Promotional Campaign for 2003.

CINGULAR WIRELESS/SALES DEPARTMENT/JANUARY 1999-MAY 2001
INSIDE SALES/ACCOUNT EXECUTIVE

Responsibilities included meeting a monthly sales quota, satisfying client needs and aggressively presenting the firms products and services of the firm. Inducted into the "100 Sub Club" three times for producing over one hundred unique customers per month (the only Account Executive in a team of forty to be inducted three times)
  - *"Team Leader"* for the Atlanta Sales Department: The "Best of the Best Competition", a company wide event that allowed teams from different departments to present their concepts of the competitive advantages of Cingular Wireless.
  - *"Innovator"*; provided cutting-edge information to the department regarding sales and marketing trends, competitor's marketing mixes, and new developments in the telecommunication industry.

- "*Researcher*"; produced a comprehensive report proposing solutions to decreasing customer migration, a industry challenge known as "churn"
- "*Professional*"; exceeded monthly sales quota for twenty six consecutive months

UPLIFT PROFESSIONAL SERVICES & MANAGEMENT, INC./ATLANTA, GA
JUNE 1994- DECEMBER 1999
FOUNDING PARTNER-CHIEF OPERATING OFFICER

Functions included developing and implementing the corporate strategy and vision for a progressive entertainment management firm. Produced, executed, and monitored the marketing strategies and plans for clients.
- Created opportunities for emerging artist to enter into contractual agreement with major recording labels
- Primary liaison between clients and entertainment industry representatives, securing live performance engagements for artist at major industry events and trade conferences
- Participated in numerous music industry conferences as a panelist addressing how the internet could be used by the recording industry to generate revenue

LEADERSHIP
❖ *Co-Chair of Finance Liaison Committee for William Ford Charity*
  o *2002-2007*

❖ *Founder of Plan-Atlanta*
  o *2003-2007*

❖ *VP of Communication American Marketing Association Young Professionals Atlanta Chapter*
  o *2004-2006*

❖ *Led-Consultant for Fan-O-Maniac Media Group*
  o *2004-2005*

EDUCATION
Kennesaw State University-Kennesaw, Georgia
Bachelor of Business Administration, Accounting

RONALD B. WOOLWORTH

4545 Littleton Ridge • Atlanta, GA 30355
(555) 552-5534 • ronaldbwoolworth@yahoo.com

BUSINESS DEVELOPMENT PROFESSIONAL

Large Enterprise Business Solutions / Media & Entertainment Industry

- **Tenacious, performance-driven Sales Leader** with more than 10 years of success in providing strategic solutions and marketing initiatives in an ever-changing, dynamic business climate.
- **Well-developed, in-depth knowledge of the entertainment and media industry**—strategic planning, marketing/promotions, retail, product management, and technological.
- **Proven record of achievement in exceeding sales goals** with rapid prospect qualification, needs analysis, solution development and ROI overview, value propositions to overcome objections, negotiations of proposal terms and conditions, deal closing, and post-sale follow-ups.
- **Technically astute, quick to learn** new product lines, technical data, and design specifications.

PROFESSIONAL EXPERIENCE

HEWLETT PACKARD COMPANY / TECHNOLOGY SOLUTIONS GROUP—Atlanta, GA

BladeSystem Industry Standard Server (ISS) Sales Specialist (2006 to Present)
Accountable for sales in two-state territory of Florida and Georgia. Focus on enterprise-wide sales to 10 key accounts, including *E-Trade, Norfolk Southern Transportation Co., Chick-fil-A, The Weather Channel,* and *InterContinental Hotels* with **annual sales quota of $5 million and overall territorial quota of $20 million.** Partner with cross-functional teams to identify, develop, qualify, and close business opportunities. Leverage sales and marketing resources to strengthen footprint with existing clients and expand account base with new clients, building loyal relationships and strategic partnerships and becoming a trusted advisor to clients.

- **Achieved more than 95% of sales goal** for entire year within five months of current fiscal year.
- **Increased business with two leading accounts by 100%;** substantially grew sales with all others.
- **Recognized for high level of fluency and depth of knowledge in area of expertise;** able to explain products in a nontechnical, easily understandable manner.
- **Use consultative/solution selling and networking skills,** becoming a trusted advisor, to influence purchasing decisions of C-level executives.
- **Initiate innovative promotional techniques to increase product awareness** and interest— including on-site training, tours of the HP facility, distribution of informational e-mails and newsletters, and coordinating logistics of special events and lunch-and-learn programs.

FAN-O-MANIAC MEDIA GROUP—Atlanta, GA

Business Development Consultant (2004 to 2006)
Led this startup marketing firm's conceptualization, development, and implementation of a major media project to market a concept for enhancing sports fans' experience with the Atlanta Falcons. Effectively targeted the "18–34" demographic by recruiting high-profile local and national sports broadcasting personalities and executives to provide ideas for and appear in a 30-minute promotional pilot.

- **Leveraged relationships to secure meetings with C-level executives** to engage their expertise in planning and appearing in the pilot; crafted marketing proposals and negotiated contracts.

MARKET SOURCE / HEWLETT-PACKARD RETAIL PROGRAM—Atlanta, GA

Territory Sales Manager (2001 to 2004)
Served as in-store sales representative of 13 retail product categories at leading computer retailers, including *Best Buy, CompUSA, Office Max, Office Depot,* and *Micro Center,* with full responsibility for sales, product placement, inventory maintenance, product training, and promotional efforts. Conducted in-store training.

Figure 4.22: After.

Ronald B. Woolworth • 555-552-5534

- ◆ **Increased sales 85%** year-over-year during tenure.
- ◆ **Winner,** *Bring It Home Tour* competition, for Best Recap/Promotional Campaign (2003).

CINGULAR WIRELESS / SALES DEPARTMENT—**Atlanta, GA**

Inside Sales / Account Executive (1999 to 2001)

Noted for consistent excellence in sales and customer service. Researched and shared cutting-edge information with peers on sales and marketing trends, competitor's marketing mixes, and new developments in the telecommunications industry. Authored comprehensive report on effective solutions to decrease the incidence of frequent customer migration.

- ◆ **Three-time inductee** into the *100 Sub Club* for producing 100 unique customers in one month—the only account executive in a team of 40 to achieve this.
- ◆ **Exceeded monthly sales quotas** for 26 consecutive months.

UPLIFT PROFESSIONAL SERVICES AND MANAGEMENT, INC.—**Atlanta, GA**

Founding Partner / Chief Operating Officer (1994 to 1999)

Developed and implemented the startup's corporate strategy and vision. Led this progressive entertainment sports management firm to high revenue growth through development of innovative marketing and promotional programs for urban professionals. Produced, executed, and monitored marketing strategies for new artists to enter into contractual agreements with major recording labels.

- ◆ **Generated $500K revenues** through independently planned and staged networking events for five consecutive years.
- ◆ **Secured live performance engagements** for artists at major industry events and trade shows.
- ◆ **Established long-term business relationships** with emerging film producers and leaders in the entertainment and media arena.
- ◆ **Secured sponsorship from industry leaders,** including *Coca-Cola, Cox Enterprise,* and *Verizon.*

AFFILIATIONS

Founder, Plan-Atlanta, strategic planning organization devoted to enhancing quality of life in Atlanta (2003–2007)

Co-Chair, Finance Liaison Committee for William Ford Charity (2002–2007)

VP of Communications, American Marketing Association Young Professionals, Atlanta Chapter (2004–2006)

EDUCATION

Bachelor of Business Administration in Accounting • Kennesaw State University, Kennesaw, GA

Resume Transformation #12: Ariel Nivens

Resume Writer:

Melissa Bermea
Real-Time Transcription and WP Services
Gilroy, CA
Phone: (408) 847-9180
E-mail: MBermea@aol.com

The Situation

Ariel was ready to move up to the next level in her sales career. She had held progressive positions in retail sales and management before moving to sales of technology-related products, and she needed a top-notch resume to compete for other computer and technology sales positions.

The "Before" Version

Heavy on job duties, this resume is inefficiently laid out and does not clearly articulate Ariel's value.

The "After" Version—Applying the Five Resume Makeover Strategies

- **Fashion a Strong Framework.** A chronological format with emphasis on job titles and achievements draws readers' attention to the most important facts of Ariel's career.

- **Start with a Superlative Summary.** Because her "after" resume is just one concise page, a lengthier summary is appropriate. It clearly points out three distinct areas of strength and accomplishment where she can add value to her next employer.

- **Emphasize Experience and Accomplishments.** Notice how numbers and achievements stand out through effective formatting and judicious editing to bring just the right information to the forefront.

- **Enhance with Education and "Extras."** Ariel's associate degree is eliminated because she has two bachelor's degrees that make the lower-level degree redundant.

- **Proofread and Polish to Perfection.** A sharp new format puts the finishing touch on Ariel's resume.

ARIEL NIVENS

555 Meridian Avenue ▪ San José, CA 95126
Phone: (408) 555-1212
arielnivens@yahoo.com

ACCOUNT MANAGER

PROFILE

- Compassionate and dedicated professional, providing utmost customer service, customer care, and expertise in the following areas:
  - o Exceeding sales gols
  - o Managing global accounts
  - o Excellent customer service
  - o Public relations skills
  - o Training
- Ten years of success in both inside and outside sales and sales management
- Proven record of managing major OEM accounts within the Semiconductor, Food Packaging, and Medical industries.
- An articulate, team player who utilizes both a strong business acumen and technological competency
- Valuable leader accentuating well-developed office techniques, strong training, and ethical work habits.
- Excellent trilingual (English, Portuguese, and Spanish) written and verbal communication.
- Proficient with MS Word and Excel, Windows applications, and the Internet.
- Humbly demonstrates courtesy, integrity, flexibility, and a positive attitude.

RELEVANT EXPERIENCE

ACCOUNTING MANAGER ....02/2005 - Present
SMC Corporation of America, San Jose, CA
- Responsible for identifying and developing new business and increasing market share in high-technology industries.
- Developing strong relationships with key contacts within the semiconductor and bio-medical industries resulting in $500k in new business.
- Maintaining long-term customer relations making SMC a preferred vender.
- Managing all aspects of customer accounts, including technical assistance, price quotes, contract negotiations, and product demonstrations.
- Communicating with various level of management, technical staff and product team to discuss customer's and expedite SMC's business process.
- Researching and introduced new products to the SMC USA pneumatic product line.

STORE MANAGER 2004-2005
Ann Taylor, Stanford Mall, Palo Alto, CA
- Responsible for operational management in a retail sales environment.
- Responsible for hire and training all new district managers.
- Hired, trained and managed sales staff.
- Consistently exceeded monthly sales goal of $400K by an average of 15%.

Figure 4.23: Before.   *(continued)*

(continued)

STORE MANAGER 2003-2004
Bebe, Valley Fair Mall, Santa Clara, CA
- Responsible for yearly sales of $5 million.
- Increased sales by over 20% annually.
- Responsible for tracking sales by product and reporting trends to regional management.
- Hired, trained and managed sales staff.

ASSISTANT MANAGER 2001-2003
Coldwater Creek, Valley Fair Mall, CA
- Lead a successful team effort to exceed $2 Million annual sales goal.
- Responsible for setting sales associates monthly sales goals.
- Assisted in developing and implementing action plans to improve team performance.

**EDUCATION/
TRAINING**

The National University	San Jose, CA	B.A. Business Administration	2008
Heald College	Milpitas, CA	A.A. Business Administration	2006
University of Paraiba	Paraiba, Brazil	B.A. Marketing	1998

ARIEL NIVENS

555 Meridian Avenue ▪ San José, CA 95126
408.222.3333 ▪ arielnivens@yahoo.com

ACCOUNT MANAGER with BUSINESS DEVELOPMENT EXPERTISE

Top sales achiever in semiconductor and related industries. More than seven years of professional experience building effective relationships, improving company growth, and discovering new potential business opportunities. Trilingual in English, Portuguese, and Spanish. **Strengths:**

❐ **SALES:** Identify products that best meet customer needs. Deliver confident presentations and aggressively close business. Increased account base from 10 accounts to 170, acquiring top-tier new business and increasing sales within existing accounts. Improved customer retention by addressing and closing critical customer issues. Resurrected and restored a large number of previously lost customers.

❐ **LEADERSHIP & MANAGEMENT:** Manage OEM accounts in semiconductor, food packaging, and medical industries; communicate solutions to their global accounts. Train and motivate new employees to strive to reach goals and objectives.

❐ **CUSTOMER SERVICE:** Foster a strong total customer experience with an expert ability to diffuse problem situations quickly. Known for strong communication style, expert customer follow-up, and a sense of humor.

EXPERIENCE & ACCOMPLISHMENTS

SMC Corporation of America, San José, CA   4/2005–present
ACCOUNT MANAGER
- Added $500K per year in new business.
- Grew account base from 10 to 170 accounts.
- Discovered 25 new accounts by sourcing and cold calling.
- Acquired top accounts: LAM Research, Novellus, Intel, and Applied Materials, with potential $1M account in pipeline.
- Resurrected 20 inactive and lost accounts, returning these customers to SMC products.

Ann Taylor, Stanford Mall, Palo Alto, CA   2/2004–4/2005
STORE MANAGER
- Exceeded monthly sales goal of $400K, averaging 15% month-over-month.
- Recruited, trained, and supervised average of 50+ employees.
- Tracked expenses to minimize loss prevention and achieve cost-effective operations.
- Processed reports and payroll.

Bebe, Valley Fair Mall, San José, CA   1/2003–2/2004
STORE MANAGER
- Met goal of $4.5M in sales, earning rank as one of the branch's sales leaders.
- Increased prior-year sales more than 15%.
- Recruited, trained, and supervised average of 40 employees.

Coldwater Creek, Valley Fair Mall, San José, CA   3/2001–1/2003
ASSISTANT MANAGER
- Led team effort to exceed $2M yearly sales goal.
- Trained new employees on floor etiquette and performance improvement.

EDUCATION & TRAINING

B.A., Business Administration   THE NATIONAL UNIVERSITY, SAN JOSE, CA (2008)
B.A., Marketing   UNIVERSITY OF PARAIBA, BRAZIL (2000)

Figure 4.24: After.

Resume Transformation #13:
John Acker

Resume Writer:

Nancy Branton, MRW, MA
People Potential Group, Inc.
8362 Tamarack Village, 119-121
Woodbury, MN 55129
Phone: (651) 459-0528
E-mail: nancy@peoplepotentialgroup.com
www.peoplepotentialgroup.com

The Situation

John was looking for a training position in the healthcare field; specifically, he was interested in and qualified to train both nurses and paraprofessional staff.

The "Before" Version

John's "before" resume is the typical CV that is often found in medical and academic fields. Although it presents his credentials, it does not say much about his skill and experience in training healthcare professionals.

The "After" Version—Applying the Five Resume Makeover Strategies

- **Fashion a Strong Framework.** John's CV was transformed into a powerful resume. A semifunctional format is used, with key functional headings, many related to training capabilities, highlighted on page 1. Pages 2 and 3 are a chronological presentation of his academic credentials and work history.

- **Start with a Superlative Summary.** John's summary describes who he is, encompassing both his nursing background and his training skills. The headline and branding statement make his focus clear, and the "Key Competencies" highlight his vast areas of expertise in both hands-on nursing and healthcare training.

- **Emphasize Experience and Accomplishments.** John's new employ-ment history details what he did in each job. The "Key Accomplishments" under his most current position emphasize his training successes as well as leadership skills.

- **Enhance with Education and "Extras."** Notice that John includes his licensure and certification on page 1 because these are essential for his field. Page 2 shows his most recent workshops and seminars, and page 3 includes his formal education and professional affiliations.

- **Proofread and Polish to Perfection.** Although it's more detailed, John's resume is shorter than his original version and presents a sharp, professional image.

John Acker

Business	Home
State University Medical Center	555 Health Drive
433 University Drive	Oakdale, MN 55128
St. Paul, MN 55155	Home: (651) 444-3333
(612) 555-4443	Cellular: (651) 444-3334
	Email: johnacker@comcast.net

EDUCATION

Graduate	University of St. Thomas, Minneapolis, MN M.B.A.	2004
Baccalaureate	College of St. Catherine, St. Paul, MN. B.S., Nursing *magna cum laude*	1996
	College of St. Catherine, St. Paul, MN. B. A., Organizational Studies *cum laude*	1993
Associate	Inver Hills Community College, Inver Grove Heights, MN. A.S., Nursing	1989
	Inver Hills Community College, Inver Grove Heights, MN. A.A.S., Paramedic	1988
	Inver Hills Community College, Inver Grove Heights, MN. A. A.	1987
	Minnesota Bible College, St. Paul, MN. General Studies (no degree sought)	1983
Vocational	916 Vocational Technical Institute, Minneapolis, MN Degree of Occupational Proficiency- Paramedic Minnesota and National Registry: EMT-Paramedic	1985
Certificate	Iowa State University, EMSLRC, Ames, IA Iowa Emergency Medical Technician-Intermediate Iowa Board of Medical Examiners Certification as EMT-I	1982
	Vocational Technical Institute Minneapolis, MN Minnesota Certified & Nationally Registered as Emergency Medical Technician-Ambulance	1981
	Iowa Community College, Ames, IA Iowa Certified Emergency Medical Technician-A	1980
	Vocational Cooperative St. Paul, MN Certified Nursing Assistant	1979

Figure 4.25: Before.

John Acker
Page Two

CURRENT LICENSURE AND CERTIFICATION

Registered Nurse	Minnesota License Number R 123654-1
	Washington License Number RN02134945
Public Health Nurse	Minnesota Registration Certificate Number 13721
Basic Cardiac Life Support for HealthCare Providers	American Heart Association
Advanced Cardiac Life Support	American Heart Association

PROFESSIONAL EXPERIENCE

RN-Cardiology /Assistant Nurse Manager	ABC University Medical Center Unit 6C/D (Telemetry) University Campus	3/2001-Present
RN-Cardiology	ABC University Medical Center Unit 6C/D (Telemetry) University Campus	12/1999-3/2001
RN-Per-diem: Home Infusion Therapy	XYZ Integrated Home Care Saint Paul, Minnesota	8/1998 – 12/1999
RN-Supervisor/ Physician's Sub.	ABC BioServices *(Previously ABC Blood Alliance)* Minneapolis, Minnesota	3/1998 - 8/1998

(continued)

(continued)

John Acker
Page Three

PROFESSIONAL EXPERIENCE *(Continued)*

RN-Case Manager: Home Infusion Therapy	XYZ Integrated Home Care Saint Paul, Minnesota	5/1997 - 3/1998 1/1996 – 10/1996
RN-Center Shift Supervisor/Apheresis	Puget Sound Blood Center Seattle, Washington	11/1996 – 5/1997
RN-Supervisor/ Physician's Sub	ABC Blood Alliance Minneapolis, Minnesota	10/1991 – 7/1996
RN/Orthopedics, Relief Charge Nurse, BCLS Instructor	Saint Paul Medical Center Saint Paul, Minnesota	7/1989 – 10/ 1991
Phlebotomist/Group Leader	ABC Blood Alliance Minneapolis, Minnesota	8/1987 – 7/1989
Personal Care Attendant	Independently (Privately) Employed *(Employer's name confidential due to Patient Privacy)* Minneapolis, Minnesota	11/1986 – 5/1989
EMT-Paramedic	DEF County Ambulance St. Paul, Minnesota	6/1986 – 9/1986
EMT-Paramedic, EMT-Ambulance, EMT Dispatcher, BCLS Instructor	GHI Ambulance *(Assets Acquired by JKL Ambulance)* St. Paul, Minnesota	11/1984 – 6/1986

John Acker
Page Four

PROFESSIONAL EXPERIENCE *(Continued)*

EMT-Ambulance, **EMT-Dispatcher**	Valley EMS, Inc. *(Assets Acquired by GHI Ambulance)* St. Paul, Minnesota	7/1984 – 11/1984
EMT-Ambulance, **BCLS Instructor**	Minnesota Regional Hospital Ambulance Service Mankato, Minnesota	9/1983 - 7/1984
EMT Ambulance, **On Call**	Minnesota Regional Hospital Ambulance Service Mankato, Minnesota	8/1981 – 1/1983
EMT-Ambulance, **Night Janitor**	Hand Memorial Hospital Ames, Iowa	7/1980 – 1/1981

Affiliations

College of St. Catherine's Nursing Honor Society-Past President

Chi-at-Large Chapter, Sigma Theta Tau

American Association of Critical Care Nurses (AACN)

Greater Twin Cities Chapter of AACN

JOHN ACKER, RN, BSN

555 Health Drive
Oakdale, MN 55128

Mobile: 555-444-3333

johnacker@comcast.net

HEALTHCARE PROFESSIONAL | NURSE TRAINER & MANAGER

More than 7 years at a nationally renowned medical facility as Assistant Nurse Manager, providing staff supervision, training, and hands-on patient care. More than 20 years of diverse healthcare experience in nursing, emergency medical services, and pre-hospital care as an EMT and paramedic.

Provided nursing care in cardiology, heart and lung transplant, advanced care, critical care, home infusion therapy, case management, orthopedics, and aphaeresis as well as therapeutic blood collection/transfusion services. Strong training and employee development, communication, problem-solving, project management, and supervision skills. Possess an MBA and a BA in organizational studies as well as a BSN.

Dependable, caring, and highly skilled professional nurse who educates and coaches staff to provide the very best hands-on nursing care to their patients.

CURRENT LICENSURE & CERTIFICATIONS

- **Registered Nurse (RN) License:** Minnesota License Number R 115587-3
- **Public Health Nurse:** Minnesota Registration Certificate Number 12731
- **Basic Cardiac Life Support** (BCLS): American Heart Association
- **Advanced Cardiac Life Support** (ACLS): American Heart Association

KEY COMPETENCIES

Design & Develop Competency-Based Training Orientation & Ongoing Training Activities
Conducted needs assessment, identified learning objectives, researched topics, developed curriculum, and evaluated training outcomes and effectiveness.

Staff Performance Improvement & Development
Conducted performance appraisals; created plans to develop staff's skills; identified performance deficiencies; collaborated to create individualized performance improvement plans; coached for skill development; created personalized competency-based training activities and supporting materials; and assessed training outcomes.

Recruit Professional & Paraprofessional Healthcare Staff
Performed targeted recruitment; conducted pre-employment screening for paraprofessional candidates; and selected staff who succeeded in their jobs.

Patient Care & Life Support Expertise
Demonstrated expertise in the following care specialties: cardiac EKG interpretation and analysis; nursing care delivery; and patient care environment management including patient assessment, patient monitoring, skilled nursing care provision, patient and family education, and patient care documentation using electronic medical record systems.

Computer Expertise
Utilized strong skills in PC and network hardware/software setup, configuration, and troubleshooting for daily operation of medical and office systems. Gained proficiency in software applications such as Microsoft Office Suite, Outlook, HIRE, E-Forms, E-Time, One-Staff, and Eclipsys-Sunrise Critical Care.

Health Care Equipment Expertise
Developed advanced expertise in patient equipment/technologies in ICU, CCU, advanced care, step-down, and general care patient care units; expert knowledge in use of telemetry monitoring systems, hardwired monitoring systems, and portable monitor/defibrillators; extensive experience in the art of safe patient lifting/transfer using patient immobilization devices, transfer devices, and a variety of lifting equipment.

Figure 4.26: After.

LEADERSHIP & STAFF DEVELOPMENT TRAINING

A Dynamic Duo: Staff Development and You, Lippincott, Williams, & Wilkins (2.5 hrs.)	2008
Tapping the Energy of Conflict, Fairview Health Services (4 hrs.)	2007
The Use of Unlicensed Assistive Personnel in the Critical Care Setting, AACN (1 hr.)	2005
Managing for Success, Fairview-University Medical Center (16 hrs.)	2004
Mentoring and Leadership Workshop, Fairview-University Medical Center (8 hrs.)	2004
Preceptor Development Workshop, Fairview-University Medical Center (8 hrs.)	2003

NURSING & HEALTH CARE EXPERIENCE

ABC UNIVERSITY MEDICAL CENTER, Minneapolis, Minnesota   1999–2008

RN-CARDIOLOGY/ASSISTANT NURSE MANAGER (2001 to 2008)
RN-CARDIOLOGY (1999 to 2001)

Supervised 60 paraprofessional staff (nursing assistants, nursing monitor technicians, health unit coordinators, nursing station technicians) and 120 nurses in the provision of medical and surgical care of critically and acutely ill patients with an emphasis on heart and lung disorders including organ transplantation. Ensured that equipment and technologies needed were available, working, and well maintained.

Key Accomplishments

- Enhanced paraprofessional skill-sets by developing and implementing a variety of unit-based employee training programs/activities and by cross-training paraprofessional staff.
- Ensured compliance with JCAH/CLIA competency requirements by planning, directing, and implementing necessary paraprofessional training and annual competency assessment activities.
- Saved $200K+ in recruitment and orientation costs through targeted hiring of paraprofessional staff and transitioning paraprofessional staff to RN positions. (2007)
- Contributed to improved employee satisfaction scores on annual surveys by using a collaborative leadership style. Improved operational efficiency of the unit by coordinating unit-based work redesign teams for paraprofessional staff during a recent remodel-redesign of Cardiac Telemetry Unit.
- Significantly reduced overtime costs by increasing core numbers of paraprofessional staff on all shifts, using a staffing-to-demand model and a revised staffing matrix incorporating increased core paraprofessional staffing.
- Substantially reduced paraprofessional staff turnover by implementing a targeted hiring program; individualizing and enhancing unit-based, new employee orientation for paraprofessionals; and initiating a scheduling preference program-alternative scheduling program.
- Maintained excellent management/labor relations by thoroughly understanding the paraprofessional contract and following a policy of exceeding contract provisions.

XYZ INTEGRATED HOME CARE, St. Paul, Minnesota   1996, 1997–1998, 1998–1999

RN-CASE MANAGER, HOME INFUSION THERAPY

Provided skilled nursing care and case management to patients whose diagnosis included diabetes, wound infection, HIV/AIDS, and cancer. The patient care environment included a variety of settings: patients' homes, independent living facilities, extended care facilities, and nursing homes. Supervised up to 5 paraprofessional staff.

ABC BIOSERVICES, Minneapolis, Minnesota   1991–1996, 1998

RN-SUPERVISOR/PHYSICIAN'S SUBSTITUTE (FDA-approved physician extender)

Supervised up to 50 technical and paraprofessional staff engaged in the collection of blood plasma from a paid donor population. Primary responsibilities included staff recruitment and selection of donor room staff, staff orientation/education, ongoing competency assessment of all staff, and donor room staff scheduling.

(continued)

(continued)

JOHN ACKER

Critical nursing responsibilities included donor suitability screening, counseling, and education regarding the donation process, testing for HIV/AIDS/Hepatitis, and responding to health and behavioral emergencies. Performed employee health assessments and managed immunization programs.

PUGET SOUND BLOOD CENTER, Seattle, Washington 1996–1997

RN-CENTER SHIFT SUPERVISOR/APHERESIS

Supervised up to 7 technical/paraprofessional staff engaged in the collection of whole blood, blood platelets, or blood plasma from a volunteer (unpaid) donor population. Occasionally, staff performed therapeutic patient procedures such as therapeutic phlebotomy for hemochromatosis and polycythemia.

ST. PAUL MEDICAL CENTER, St. Paul, Minnesota 1989–1991

RN/CHARGE NURSE—ORTHOPEDICS

Provided skilled nursing care and supervised shifts of approximately 4 paraprofessional staff (nursing assistants, health unit coordinators) and 7 nurses who provided medical and surgical nursing care to acutely ill/injured patients with an emphasis on caring for persons who experienced multiple traumas, orthopedic injuries, and head injuries. Team-taught basic life support/CPR to patient care unit staff.

ABC BIOSERVICES, Minneapolis, Minnesota 1987–1989

PHLEBOTOMIST/GROUP LEADER

Coordinated the activities of technical and paraprofessional staff engaged in blood plasma collection from a paid donor population. Primary responsibility to provide excellent customer service and patient care for donors, while ensuring compliance with FDA/CLIA and corporate regulations. Provided lead work direction to technical/paraprofessional staff, and responded to medical/behavioral emergencies by providing treatment based on protocols or at the direction of a physician or RN supervisor. Worked with managers and staff to ensure an effective transition from the utilization of manual blood plasma collection processes to the use of automated (plasmapheresis) plasma collection.

OTHER RELEVANT EXPERIENCE

EMT PARAMEDIC/DISPATCHER for a variety of ambulance services (6+ years)

EDUCATION

MBA—*Cardinal Stritch University, Milwaukee, WI*	2004
BSN—Nursing, *Bethel College, magna cum laude, Arden Hills, MN*	1996
BA—Organizational Studies, *Bethel College, cum laude, Arden Hills, MN*	1993
AS—Nursing, *Lakewood Community College, White Bear Lake, MN*	1989
AAS—Paramedic, *Lakewood Community College, White Bear Lake, MN*	1988
AA—*Lakewood Community College, White Bear Lake, MN*	1987
Degree of Occupational Proficiency-Paramedic—*916 Vocational Technical Institute, White Bear Lake, MN*	1985

PROFESSIONAL AFFILIATIONS

Minneapolis Chapter, Sigma Theta Tau
American Association of Critical Care Nurses (AACN)
Greater Twin Cities Chapter of AACN
Infusion Nurses Society (INS)

Resume Transformation #14: Mayela Smith

Resume Writer:

Melissa Bermea
Real-Time Transcription and WP Services
Gilroy, CA
Phone: (408) 847-9180
E-mail: MBermea@aol.com

The Situation

Mayela wanted to transition from primarily a receptionist role into sales, but her job search had stalled because potential employers could not make the connection between her experience and her goal.

The "Before" Version

Mayela did have some sales-related experience, and she clearly had the attributes needed to be successful in sales. However, her resume did not convey her value or position her as a competitive candidate.

The "After" Version—Applying the Five Resume Makeover Strategies

- **Fashion a Strong Framework.** Still formatted on one page, Mayela's new resume presents clearly organized material that lets readers quickly skim to find key information.

- **Start with a Superlative Summary.** The "Highlights" section of Mayela's new resume is a nice summary of her capabilities and qualifications.

- **Emphasize Experience and Accomplishments.** Mayela's experience is presented in such a way that readers can see the relevance to her goal of a sales position.

- **Enhance with Education and "Extras."** The left column of this resume presents many "extras" that truly enhance the picture of Mayela's qualifications, yet the resume remains extremely easy to skim.

- **Proofread and Polish to Perfection.** An arresting format will draw employers' attention, and the great content will keep them reading!

Mayela Smith

1234 Calabra Street
SAN JOSE, CA 95148

(408)321-1234 (c)
good_day@yahoo.com

Objective

To obtain a sales account opportunity utilizing my education and experience in order to be able to contribute my knowledge in the sales industry and further build my professional career.

Personal Qualities

Detailed-oriented; able to prioritize and reach objectives
Professional management skills
Excellent customer service and costumer relation skills
Fluent in English and Spanish

Skills:

C.P.R.	Typing 35 wpm
C.M.A.	Microsoft Word
Monetary Collections	Microsoft Excel
Transcription	Alpha & Digit Filing
Scan, Fax, & Copy	Documentation
Power Point	Management Concepts
Outlook	Organization of Work Flow
Data Entry	Bilingual English/Spanish

Experience and Duties

Receptionist/ Phone Operator   *Jan Marini Skin Research, San Jose, CA*   *2006-Present*
Operation of the switchboard handling heavy call volumes in addition to promptly and professionally transferring and directed calls.
Organized, tracked, and filed large amounts of invoices in an accurate manner in order to efficiently retrieve information to co-workers.
Structured numeral amounts of Info-Packs for prospects and current customers.
Provided customers with cosmetic information and special offers.

Receptionist/ D.A.   *Dr. Sepulveda, San Jose, CA*   *2004-2006*
Scheduled appointments answered and directed incoming phone calls.
Ordered and stocked supplies, processed mail & distribution of mail.
Gave procedure and insurance consultations to patients and acquired pre-authorizations.
Collection of cash, data entry, filing, photo copying, e-mails, inventory, faxing.
Assisted the doctor with all procedures.
Met and exceeded all corporation objectives within deadlines by using all available organizational resources.

Sales Floor Associate   *Rampage, Santa Clara, CA*   *2003-2004*
Met and exceeded all corporation objectives and sales quotas within deadlines.
Aggressively achieved and stretched goals on a monthly basis
Function of computer register for purchases, returns, and discounts.
Promoted store specials and clothing in order to increase sales potential.

Education

Administration	San Jose Ca.
Business Administration	Class of 2009

Figure 4.27: Before.

MAYELA SMITH

1234 Cabala Street
San José, CA 95123

408.321.1234
mayela_smith@yahoo.com

CAPABILITIES

- Communications
- Organization Efficiency
- Outgoing Sales Mentality
- Independence / Teamwork
- Leadership Concepts
- Customer Rapport / Etiquette
- Enthusiasm / Self-Motivation
- First Impression Excellence
- Resourceful / Network Ability
- Consistent & Focused
- Work to Exceed Quotas
- Multitasker / Project-Oriented
- Attention to Detail
- Informative / Go-To Appointee
- Heavy Scheduling
- Creative in Designing
- Database / Inventory Management
- Project Follow-Through / Deadlines
- Natural Grace under Pressure

EDUCATION

B.S., Business Management
University of Phoenix (anticipated 2010)

A.S., Administration
Heald Business College (2006)

SOFTWARE

MS Office (Word, Excel, PowerPoint, Outlook), Adobe Acrobat (pdf), Webex, Internet Research

LANGUAGES

Bilingual in English and Spanish

(Flexible for Travel)

SALES ASSOCIATE—Entry Level

Instant Customer Rapport | Sales Stamina | Customer Service

HIGHLIGHTS

- ❑ Sales experience and enthusiasm to progress further within sales environment.
- ❑ Eager to learn new concepts; a self-starter and quick learner.
- ❑ Punctual—arrive early every day and work hard to fulfill goals/quotas.
- ❑ Reputation for "excellent first impression" and "informative and helpful" mannerism.
- ❑ Ability to interact with diverse individuals; appointed to work with "those most difficult."
- ❑ Crisis-management skills.
- ❑ Bilingual in English and Spanish.
- ❑ A.S. degree; working to achieve B.S. in Business Management (expected 2010).

EXPERIENCE

Jan Marini Skin Research, San José, CA 2006–present
RECEPTIONIST / PHONE OPERATOR (SALES ENVIRONMENT)
- ▪ Administer heavy 12-line phone operation with professional etiquette.
- ▪ Inform and direct internal/external customers appropriately.
- ▪ Manage schedule of agendas, meetings, and conferences.
- ▪ Systemize and maintain tracking of invoices.
- ▪ Provide resourceful Internet research; retrieve information for executives.
- ▪ Organize and mail information packets and company pamphlets.
- ▪ Provide ad hoc assistance for back-office sales professionals.
- ▪ Created a company log sheet used for tracking purposes.
- ▪ Keep a well-organized front desk area at all times.

Amos Sepulveda, DDS, San José, CA 2004–2006
RECEPTIONIST / DENTAL ASSISTANT
- ▪ Handled heavy phone line with proper etiquette and care.
- ▪ Managed inventory control, processed mail, and distributed correspondence.
- ▪ Provided procedure/insurance consultation for clients; acquired pre-authorizations.
- ▪ Met and exceeded all deadline objectives utilizing available resources.
- ▪ Responded quickly and effectively to all internal/external inquiries.
- ▪ Scheduled and organized conferences and meetings.
- ▪ Performed monetary collections, data entry, filing, photocopying, faxing, and e-mail distribution.

Rampage, Santa Clara, CA 2003–2004
SALES ASSOCIATE
- ▪ Met and exceeded an average of 15%–20% monthly sales goals.
- ▪ Aggressively achieved and monthly stretch goals.
- ▪ Developed quick rapport with customers.
- ▪ Ensured excellent level of customer service at all times.
- ▪ Built strong relationships and worked well with team members.
- ▪ Promoted store specials and clothing to increase sales potential.
- ▪ Operated register for purchases and returns.
- ▪ Assisted in staging storefront and maintained clean floor environment.

Figure 4.28: After.

Resume Transformation #15: Hazel Reyes

Resume Writer:

Melissa Bermea
Real-Time Transcription and WP Services
Gilroy, CA
Phone: (408) 847-9180
E-mail: MBermea@aol.com

The Situation

Having just completed a graduate degree in Human Resources, Hazel wanted to transition from the financial services industry into a role as a corporate HR manager.

The "Before" Version

Hazel's original resume focused strongly on her financial services experience and did not position her for her current goal. In fact, it included very little mention of her highly relevant human resources activities.

The "After" Version—Applying the Five Resume Makeover Strategies

- **Fashion a Strong Framework.** A chronological format was used to show Hazel's extensive business background in significant leadership roles.

- **Start with a Superlative Summary.** Hazel's new resume begins with a highly targeted headline and continues with a summary of her relevant experience and knowledge to position her for human resources leadership roles.

- **Emphasize Experience and Accomplishments.** Within each position, the activities and accomplishments that are emphasized relate primarily to human resources activities.

- **Enhance with Education and "Extras."** Compare the Education section of Hazel's "before" resume to the "after" version. You can see that irrelevant education has been omitted and her recent advanced education is highlighted. A summary of technical skills rounds out the resume.

- **Proofread and Polish to Perfection.** Professional and eye-catching, the appearance of Hazel's new resume is a match for her professional goals.

777 Mt. Olive Street
Hollister, CA 95023
(408) 555-5555
hazel_professional@hotmail.com

Hazel Reyes

Qualifications	20 years successful experience in the securities industry.
	Extensive experience in the start-up and operation of local independent brokerage/money management company.
	Computer Literate.
	Motivated and enthusiastic about developing good relations with clients.
	Professional appearance, presentation and communication.

Experience	1995-Present PruneYard Financial Group Campbell, CA
	Operations Manager / Retirement Plan Specialist
	• Involved with start-up and operations of Registered Investment Advisor.
	• Professional assistance to clients.
	• Manage reconciliation, analysis and reporting of investment advisory data to investors and regulatory firms.
	• Assist with administration of 401(k) and other retirement plans.
	• Operational activities include: marketing, payroll, human resources and computer database management responsibilities.
	1986-1995 Everen Securities, Inc. Santa Clara, CA
	Registered Sales Assistant
	• Assist investment executives with planning and prioritizing daily activities.
	• Problem solving, client communication.
	• Stock option exercise and Rule 144 transaction processing.
	• Trade Processing.
	1983-1986 Bradford Securities, Inc. Fort Lee, NJ
	Bond Conversion Specialist
	• Operations surrounding conversation of convertible subordinate debentures to common stock.

Figure 4.29: Before.   *(continued)*

(continued)

- Compiling and submitting corporate financial reports to corporations and corporate administrators.
- Reconciliation and monies involving cash-in-lieu of fractional shares.
- Communication with registered representatives and individual shareholders about conversions.
- Maintain computer database.

1978-1980   Dean Witter Reynolds, Inc.   New York, N.Y.
Mutual Fund Trade Adjuster
- Adjustments to mutual fund purchase and sales transactions.
- Telephone, written and wire communication with banks, brokers and individual investors.

Education

2007-Present University of Phoenix, San José, CA
- Masters, Human Resources

1999 University of Phoenix, San José, CA
- B.S. Business Administration

1994
Series 7
Series 63

1979-1981 Rutgers University, Newark, NJ
1975-1977 Cambridge University diploma, Couva, Trinidad, W.I.

Interests

Running, Writing Poetry

HAZEL REYES

408.555.5555
hazel_reyes@hotmail.com
777 Mt. Olive Street, Hollister, CA 93000

HR CORPORATE MANAGER
Employee Relations • Recruitment & Training • Operations Management

*Visionary leader who aligns superior competence, initiative, commitment,
and strategies with company goals and objectives*

HR generalist with proven leadership skills in all aspects of human resources as well as operations management and extensive experience with retirement/investment planning and risk/expense management.

Business strategist with global experience/communication skills and both startup and established company background. MBA in Human Resources and BS in Business Administration. *Career highlight:* Instrumental in growth of startup to $220M in assets through strategic, operational, and HR leadership.

CAPABILITIES

Recruitment/Hiring/Terminations	State & Federal Laws & Regulations	Constructive Teaching/Training
Policies/Procedures Development	Risk/Change Management	Data Administration/Confidentiality
Benefits/Compensation/Stock Options	Issue Resolution Guidance	Influence & Negotiation
Budget Management/Prioritization	Leadership & Division of Labor	Project Management & Follow-Through

---

EXPERIENCE

PruneYard Financial Group, Campbell, CA..1995–present

OPERATIONS MANAGER—RETIREMENT PLAN SPECIALIST (HR)

Integral in growing startup company to $220M in assets under management. Member of executive team, setting strategy for the business and making both long-term and day-to-day business decisions. Created all operational policies and procedures.

- Administer human resources, payroll, marketing, and database discretion.

- Engage full process of employee recruitment/terminations.

- Lead staff to strengthen business partner relationships and issue resolution.
  - Develop goals and division of labor among employees.
  - Prioritize and direct strategies as required; create incentive programs.

- Provide 401(k), Roth IRA, mutual funds, and various retirement plan assistance.

- Structure budget organization for participants and provide financial guidance.

- Serve national participants to achieve sound retirement and creative opportunities.

- Manage reconciliation, analysis, and reporting of investment issuance.

- Strategize areas of needed improvement in height of economy change.

Figure 4.30: After.   *(continued)*

(continued)

HAZEL REYES
408.555.5555
hazel_reyes@hotmail.com
Page 2

Everen Securities, Santa Clara, CA...1986–1995
REGISTERED SALES ASSISTANT
- Served executives and financial advisors with efficient planning and prioritizing.
- Administered stock option exercise and Rule 144 transaction processing.
- Handled inquiries and critical problem-solving issues for clientele.
- Prepared correspondence, forms, and spreadsheet requirements.
- Conducted trade processing, allowing for verification and reconciliation.

Bradford Securities, Inc., Fort Lee, NJ...1983–1986
BOND CONVERSION SPECIALIST
- Conducted operations surrounding conversion of convertible subordinate debentures to common stock.
- Compiled financial reports to corporations and corporate administrators.
- Performed reconciliation of monies involving cash-in-lieu of fractional shares.
- Communicated information with registered representatives and shareholders.
- Maintained computer database and confidential material.

EDUCATION

MBA, Human Resources
University of Phoenix, San José, CA (2008)

BS, Business Administration
University of Phoenix, San José, CA (1999)

Registered Securities Representative
Series 7 and Series 63 Licensed

TECHNOLOGY SKILLS

MS Suite (Word, Excel, PowerPoint, Outlook),
Adobe/Acrobat, Lacerte, Portfolio Center, and Internet Research

Resume Transformation #16: Mark Stanford

Resume Writer:

Nancy Branton, MRW, MA
People Potential Group, Inc.
8362 Tamarack Village, 119-121
Woodbury, MN 55129
Phone: (651) 459-0528
E-mail: nancy@peoplepotentialgroup.com
www.peoplepotentialgroup.com

The Situation

Mark had lost his job when the upheaval in the mortgage industry created an impossible environment for the startup company he had joined just a year ago. As a technology executive in the financial services sector, Mark had a wealth of experience and accomplishments that he wanted to convey as he looked for a similar position.

The "Before" Version

Overly long and detailed, Mark's four-page "before" resume not only is filled with jargon, it is dense and difficult to read. Also, his most notable achievements occurred earlier in his career, and with this format it is easy for readers to miss these important accomplishments.

The "After" Version—Applying the Five Resume Makeover Strategies

- **Fashion a Strong Framework.** A chronological format works best for Mark because he has relevant and recent experience and is searching for jobs that are similar to those he has held throughout his career.

- **Start with a Superlative Summary.** Page 1 of Mark's new resume presents key information in an easy-to-skim format. A headline and branding statement clearly define "who he is," and the "Highlights" section allows him to place those notable achievements on page 1 so that they will not be overlooked.

- **Emphasize Experience and Accomplishments.** To help Mark achieve his goal of a technology leadership position, both technical and management activities and achievements are included. His resume is still quite detailed, but unnecessary material has been trimmed and the accomplishments are focused on the results he was able to achieve.

- **Enhance with Education and "Extras."** Mark has just a Bachelor's degree, not the advanced degree that other CIO candidates might have, but his professional training and CPA credential will help him stand out.

- **Proofread and Polish to Perfection.** A new font and subtle formatting enhancements make this resume more concise and attractive without detracting from its readability.

Mark Stanford
2222 Lake Drive, St. Paul, MN 55155 555-555-5555, 555-555-4444 (cell)
Stanfordmc@comcast.net

Summary

Senior level executive with extensive practical knowledge of the financial services industry combined with the ability to conceive of and execute business strategies via the intelligent application of technology.

Profile

- In-depth expertise in conception, design and implementation of financial services computing and telephony solutions (3 financial services start-ups, 150+ branches/call centers).
- Extensive knowledge of financial services business processes and track record of applying technologies that make high business impact.
- Seasoned in management of large projects, groups and annual budgets (> $30M combined expense and capital budgets, 80 employees, 1,500 people trained).
- Proven ability to evaluate and implement new technology standards including revolving credit, imaging, Credit Scoring, CTI, IVR/VRU, OCR, CRM, Call Monitoring systems amongst others. All of the above supported hundreds and in some cases, thousands of end users.
- Skilled in contract negotiations, delivering cost effective agreements and rapid, innovative results.
- Extensive experience in vendor collaboration and management in order to successfully customize business applications.
- Strong financial background; public accounting (CPA) & internal audit.

Experience

April, 2007-February, 2008 Lender Settlement Services (LLSS)
Chief Operating Officer
LSS was a start-up Title Insurance and Settlement Services entity that began operations in February, 2007. In April, 2007 the organization had no business process automation, no integration with vendors and 3 different operating platforms none of which were integrated to one another.

Results:
- Working with 1 web developer in 60 days integrated old website with all vendors, all clients, created automated business rules defining product, state and in some cases county level business rules and flows.
- Developed weighted evaluation criterion (125+) for new, single source system to underlie all aspects of business (May-June, 2007).
- Within chosen new system, defined over 10,000 parameters for client pricing, vendor pricing, vendor business processes, products, policy #s, state level rules, county level rules etc.
- Conducted over 75 Webex training sessions for internal personnel, clients and vendors on new system.
- Deployed system for the processing of all Title Commitments, Title Policies (October, 2007) and disbursements (January, 2008).
- Closed loans in April, 2007=60, Closed loans in January, 2008=170 with no staff increases.
- Monthly IT costs old system=$4,500/month, Monthly IT costs new system=$300/month.
- Tested ALL new enhancements, deployment of new products, new clients; in many cases was the sole tester of these components.

September, 2006-April, 2007   **Denver Mortgage Services**
Vice President-Functional Architecture

Figure 4.31: Before.   (continued)

(continued)

In 2004, Denver Mortgage had begun a major effort ($100M+) to replace its origination systems. The scope of this effort was to include all technologies and processes underlying underwriting, loan processing, closing, funding, post-closing operations. Hired because of my extensive analytical and deployment experiences with LOS, imaging and workflow systems.

Results:
- Designed and documented 10+ critical business processes underlying wholesale lending.
- Participated in technical architecture discussions as to how these business processes should be created technically.
- Developed and maintained log of detailed issues pertaining to the deployment of the new system's version supporting wholesale lending.

June, 2003 – May, 2006   Midwest Consumer Finance Americas (MCFA), Home Finance Division
Vice President of Information Technology/CIO

With a $9M budget, personally chartered to define, develop, and deploy all necessary technologies and a substantial portion of the business processes for MCFA's launch of a retail mortgage business. Started with a team of 2 resources; grew and ultimately led 22 resources to launch business.

MCFA sought to expand its financial services offerings to include a retail mortgage channel. In order to support an effective cross-sell based approach across MCFA's 44 million consumer customers, a key requirement was the selection and implementation of a new technology infrastructure that could interact with a multitude of systems. Key components included the deployment of two different middleware packages, a loan origination system, an automated underwriting capability, an automated lead management and an automated document preparation system. In addition, deep integration was required with 2 vendor management organizations to order, follow-up and fulfill appraisal, title, flood and closing transactions all while adhering to rigid security criteria. Additionally, an automated document preparation and loan servicing provider and their platforms had to be integrated as well. The technology components supported 525 users and would have easily support many multiples of that based on the effectiveness of the business processes and scalability of the architecture.

Results:
- Led selection and deployment of Mortgage Loan Origination System (LOS)
  - Performed Needs analysis and comparative analyses of multiple vendors
  - Validated vendor specifications and capabilities
  - Proposed and gained ratification of final vendor selection: MortgageFlex
  - After major business process as well as customization, LOS, Lead Management system and all critical interfaces deployed in just 110 days.
- Led "One Call" project-objective was to provide multiple loan proposals including closing costs, overall savings and an automated loan decision on 1st call to facilitate customer commitment.
  - Upgraded to MortgageFlex '04 release including "Deal Structuring"
  - Integration of LOS with Automated Underwriting (AU)
    - ❖ Real-time access of MortgageFlex data via Vitria with AU engine
    - ❖ Target automated loan approval percentage is 60% with 100% of responses delivered to the customer within 25 seconds
- Led integration of five disparate customer databases with comprehensive new loan mortgage lead management application-all integrations, completed within 9 months, are real-time (voice & data).
- Led selections and integrations of 3rd party document preparation & vendor management (appraisal, title, closing & flood certification services) companies.
  - Developed detailed criteria for both selections
  - Led business and technical design teams for both (implemented in 75 days).
  - Forced integration of vendors to one another (distribution and bar coding of closing packages).

➤ Led deployment of Nice Call Monitoring package in 1 location-68% productivity improvement vs. previous process and technology.

June 1998 - May 2003   **Baker: Mortgage and Private Label Retail Services**
Vice President of Information Systems

As a consultant and as VP of IS, responsible for strategic technical direction and application development of the home mortgage and retail services infrastructure brought to Baker through the Rock acquisition.

Developed and managed up to $8.7M capital budget and operating budgets of $23M+. Key initiatives included implementing CRM & and CTI systems to strengthen financial services product lines, and establishing a Vendor Management Company to increase real estate related profits.

Results:
➤ Implementation of Customer Relationship Management (CRM) and Computer Telephony Integration (CTI) applications.
    ❖ Negotiated Siebel CRM solution contract and participated in implementation.
    ❖ Negotiated and Implemented Genesys Computer Telephony Integration solution.
➤ Establishment of new Vendor Management Company-objective was to capture the profits on ancillary real estate products (appraisals, title works, closings etc.) by creating their own real estate vendor management company (VMC).
    ❖ Created detailed business and technical requirements for this new entity.
    ❖ Conducted extensive evaluations of competitive solutions.
    ❖ Led team of 25 resources that delivered an integrated solution to allow electronic ordering and fulfillment of appraisals, flood certifications, titles and closing/settlement services. 6,000 hour solution was delivered on time and on budget.
    ❖ Implemented an automated series of processes involving the retrieval, distribution, transformation and exchange of data and images between Baker and ZC Sterling to enable Baker to outsource its escrow and real estate tax service processes.
➤ Led team that converted paper based Lead Management system to an electronic approach in 75 days.

August 2000 – October 2001   **Business Technology Consultant**

Consulted independently, generating $330K in revenue in 15 months
Projects included:
➤ America Bank-pricing and product configuration engine: Performed analysis and prepared detailed recommendation including medium level functional requirements, analysis of products in marketplace and critical infrastructure required for project.
➤ Beverage Cola-performed detailed functional and technical analysis of competing CRM (Epiphany vs. Siebel) and CTI (Genesys vs. Avaya) alternatives.
➤ MyServ-developed a choice of alternative business models to support entry of Loan Origination System product into Managed Service Provider (MSP) market.

Sept 1995 – June 1998   **Rock Financial/Baker Finance**
Vice President, Information Systems

Key member of five person management team that developed business and technology platforms that enabled Rock (and later Baker) to enter the private label credit card (PLCC) and mortgage industries. These businesses were further expanded after acquisition by Baker and at their peak had assets of $3.2B and $13.1B, respectively. The former business had a Return on Assets (ROA) of 4.2% vs. an industry average of 2.5-3.0%.

Responsible for solution conception, vendor selection, development of success metrics, as well as driving implementation and delivery of both applications and infrastructure. The completed technology

(continued)

(continued)

enabled Rock to start and substantially grow these new businesses. Key initiatives included a new loan origination system, mortgage imaging, deployment of an outsourced credit card platform and multiple point-of-sale credit application systems.

Results:
- Management responsibility for outsourcing relationship that supplied credit card technology platform and services. Relationship grew to $20M+ in annualized expenses.
- Led team that acquired and deployed all branch technology including telecom, data networking, computing and infrastructure for 158 branches in 3 1/2 years.
- Deployed mortgage loan origination system to over 76 branches (1,500+ FTE) that originated over $4.0B in loans by 1999. Project duration from contract signing to final branch deployment was 1 year and 1 week. Ultimately, 158 branches used this system to originate loans. Total project cost was $4.5M.
- Managed personnel that planned and executed eight conversions (with six different systems/processors) in an 18-month period totaling over $215M and 510,000 accounts. Lead-time in none of these conversions was >90 days and four were done < 60 days.
- Led teams that developed Credit Card Application processing capabilities for the following platforms: Fax-in/Fax-out OCR/ICR, HyperCom, Verifone, DataCard. These platforms produced > 4M applications over a 4 year period. Approximately 80% of credit decisions rendered automatically and in < 20 seconds.
- Led teams that developed interfaces to numerous retailer (standard and homegrown) Point Of Sale systems.
- Cost justified and directed four major projects to create an integrated mortgage imaging and document tracking system used at 158 locations (branches and service centers). By the end of 2001, more than 150M imaging pages stored and available.
- Deployed 1st Voice Response Unit . Grew from 1 division, 48 port system to 336 port 5 division system processing 750,000 calls/month. 9 distinct, functional applications.

May 1988 – September 1995   **Home International**
Business Operations Manager

Originally hired as an internal operations auditor (15 months). Chose a less traditional path and entered the core business operations of the Private Label Credit Card division of Home International (Home Retail Services Inc.).

- Workflow project manager. Wrote 90+ page Cost/Benefit Analysis to secure $9.7M in capital. Redesigned processes and introduced automation to improve operating procedures, identifying 135 opportunities.
- Operations Manager. Managed customer service, loan funding, operations accounting, merchant audit and administrative services.
- Managed conversion to imaging of document retrieval system; increased document locate rate by 52%.

January 1986 – May 1988   **Hanson, Ashley and Larson**
Public Accounting auditor

Examined & analyzed the accounting & financial records for clients in the real estate, manufacturing and distribution industries.

Education
1985	B.S. Accounting. Northeastern University, Boston, MA
1989	Certified Public Accountant- CPA.

Awards
1999	Received Shimek Information Process Innovation Award (2nd place).

MARK STANFORD

2222 Lake Drive
St. Paul, MN 55100

612-555-5555
stanfordmc@comcast.net

CHIEF INFORMATION OFFICER

An innovative executive with a strong sense of urgency who collaborates with others to proactively deliver high-caliber and on-time technology solutions that significantly impact business results.

More than 15 years of experience managing large IT projects and groups—up to $30M annual budget, 80 staff, and 1,500 people trained. Proven ability to evaluate and implement highly scaleable technology solutions. High skill level in developing and maintaining solid relationships with executives, business partners, and vendors. Track record of recruiting, selecting, managing, and retaining great staff (including off-shore staff). Excellent analytical, problem-solving, negotiation, and systems-thinking skills to address strategic and tactical business needs. Strong financial background in public accounting (CPA) and internal audit.

Technology Competencies	Management Competencies
• Vendor Collaboration & Management	• Complex Contract Negotiations
• Large-scale Software Development & Implementation	• Continuous Process Improvement & Automation
• Competing Solutions—Evaluation & Matching to Complex Business Needs	• Organizational Agility
• Sophisticated Application of Testing Tools & Approaches	• Large Group Presentations
• Systems Upgrades & Conversions	• Budget Development & Management Acumen
	• Team Development

HIGHLIGHTS OF EXECUTIVE & TECHNOLOGY ACCOMPLISHMENTS

➢ Played a key management role in building two startup businesses into organizations with $3.2B and $13.1B in assets and 3,200+ employees; selected all technology applications used by employees. *(Rock/Baker)*

  • Launched a $4.5M mortgage loan origination system. *Results:* In 5 years, users originated $17B+ in assets that generated cumulative net income of $310M+; delivered all phases under budget.
  • Led $500K in point-of-sale integrations. *Results:* In 5 years generated 4M+ in applications and $1.2B in assets, with a 4% return and a cumulative net income of $48M.
  • Conceived and led implementation of credit application and loan funding automation project through application of fax-in/out, OCR, and imaging technologies ($1.7M). *Results:* In 15 months, increased productivity by 45%, resulting in $900K annual savings. Project earned second place in the Shimek Information Process Innovation Award. To date, system has funded $1.6B+ in loan volume.
  • Spearheaded rapid conversions of 8 portfolio acquisitions ($215M) in < 90 days (2 in < 30 days) at a cumulative cost of $1.1M. *Results:* Incremental annual net income of $7M+.

➢ Conceived, initiated, and implemented from scratch a cutting-edge series of integrated systems to support mortgage origination from cradle to grave. *Results:* Division achieved 75%+ higher productivity for underwriting, loan processing, and compliance than two competing divisions. By a significant margin, division had a lower percentage and number of noncompliant loans than two competing divisions. *(MCFA)*

➢ Wrote cost/benefit analysis to secure $9.7M in capital funding for workflow and imaging project. Identified 135+ process improvements and automation opportunities. *(Home International)*

EXECUTIVE EXPERIENCE & VALUE ADDED

LENDER SETTLEMENT SERVICES (LSS)—Minneapolis, MN   2007–2008
Startup title insurance and settlement services entity.

CHIEF OPERATING OFFICER
Recruited to build, integrate, upgrade, and maintain all information systems and processes.

➢ Deployed system for the processing of all title commitments, title policies, and disbursements; reduced monthly IT costs by 93%.
➢ Within chosen new system, defined 10K+ parameters for pricing, processes, products, and policies.
➢ In 60 days, integrated old website with all vendors and clients and created automated business rules that defined product, state, and county-level business rules and flows.
➢ Developed weighted evaluation criterion for new, single source system to underlie all aspects of business.

Figure 4.32: After.   *(continued)*

(continued)

DENVER MORTGAGE SERVICES—Denver, CO   2006–2007
Largest originator and servicer of residential mortgages in the U.S., with 55,000 employees.

VICE PRESIDENT, FUNCTIONAL ARCHITECTURE
Chosen to design specific business processes and underlying systems for new origination technology platform.

➤ Designed and documented 10+ critical business processes underlying wholesale lending.
➤ Participated in technical architecture discussions regarding the creation of critical business processes.

MIDWEST CONSUMER FINANCE AMERICAS: HOME FINANCE DIVISION—St. Paul, MN   2003–2006
This startup division was created to make direct loans of home mortgages to consumers; it grew to 525+ FTE.

CIO & VICE PRESIDENT, INFORMATION TECHNOLOGY
Selected by President of new division to define, develop, and deploy all necessary technologies and substantial portions of the business processes for launch of a retail mortgage business. Defined and managed a $9M capital budget and grew team from 2 to 22 members to launch the business. Deployed 3 external packages, integrated 4 critical real-estate service providers, and negotiated contracts for internal lead management system. All of these components had to be rapidly evaluated and deployed while adhering to stringent, yet frequently changing security requirements.

➤ Led selection and deployment of mortgage loan origination system. Performed needs analysis and comparative analyses of multiple vendors in 30 days; validated vendor specifications and capabilities; and, within 6 months, became one of few paperless U.S. mortgage lenders. Deployed system (MortgageFlex) in 110 days with all detailed business processes that required customizations of LOS, Lead Management system, and all critical interfaces.
➤ Led integration of five disparate customer databases, and internally developed a new and comprehensive loan mortgage lead management application; all integrations were completed within 9 months. Technology components supported 525 users and would have easily supported many multiples of that, based on the effectiveness of the business processes and scalability of the architecture.
➤ Led selections and integrations of third-party document preparation and vendor management companies.
➤ Led "One Call" project with objective to provide borrower with multiple loan proposals including closing costs, overall savings, and an automated loan decision on first call to facilitate borrower commitment. Included real-time integration to automated underwriting engine; achieved response time of < 12 seconds vs. goal of 20. Project resulted in a 20% improvement in loan officer productivity.
➤ Led collaboration and deployment of automated barcoding solution for signed closing packages between three vendors. Project resulted in the elimination of two vendor FTEs, one internal FTE, and an error reduction rate from 16% to less than 1%.
➤ Led selection and deployment of Nice Call Monitoring package in 1 location that was completed in 60 days, from contract signing to production deployment; resulted in 68% productivity improvement from previous process and technology.
➤ In 2004–2005, led implementation of 120+ projects of various sizes.

BAKER, MORTGAGE & PRIVATE LABEL RETAIL SERVICES—Eagan, MN   1998–2000, 2001–2003
A diversified provider of consumer lending products. Mortgage & Private Label divisions employed 3,200.
VICE PRESIDENT, INFORMATION SYSTEMS
As a consultant and as VP of IS, responsible for strategic technical direction and application development of the home mortgage and retail services infrastructure brought to Baker through the Rock acquisition.

Developed and managed up to $8.7M capital budget and operating budgets of $23M+. Key initiatives included implementing CRM and CTI systems to strengthen financial services product lines, and establishing a Vendor Management Company to increase real estate–related profits.

➤ Established a new vendor management company to capture profits on ancillary real estate transactions including appraisals, title works, and closings.
  • Created detailed business and technical requirements for new entity.
  • Conducted extensive evaluations of competitive solutions.
  • Led team of 25 resources that delivered an integrated solution to allow electronic ordering and fulfillment of appraisals, flood certifications, titles, and closing/settlement services. Delivered a 6,000-hour solution on time and on budget.

- Implemented an automated series of processes involving the retrieval, distribution, transformation, and exchange of data and images between Baker and Zicom to enable Baker to outsource its escrow and real estate tax service processes.
➤ Negotiated and implemented CRM (Siebel) and CTI (Genesys) applications.
➤ Led team that converted paper-based Lead Management system to an electronic approach in 75 days.

INDEPENDENT CONSULTANT—Woodbury, MN   2000–2001
Privately held company.

BUSINESS TECHNOLOGY CONSULTANT
Consulted independently, generating $330K in revenue in 15 months. Project highlights:

➤ America Bank: pricing and product configuration engine.
➤ Beverage Cola: detailed functional and technical analysis of competing CRM (Epiphany vs. Siebel) and CTI (Genesys vs. Avaya) alternatives.
➤ MyServ: alternative business models to support entry of loan origination system product into managed service provider market.

ROCK FINANCIAL/BAKER FINANCE—St. Paul, MN   1995–1998
A diversified provider of consumer lending products. Mortgage & Private Label divisions totaled 3,200 employees.

VICE PRESIDENT, INFORMATION SYSTEMS
Responsible for solution conception, vendor selection, and development of success metrics as well as driving implementation and delivery of both applications and infrastructure. The completed technology platforms enabled Rock (and later Baker) to start and substantially grow these new businesses.

➤ Managed relationship with provider of outsourced credit card platform that grew from ZERO accounts to 5M+ and a budget that grew from $100,000/month to > $2,000,000/month.
➤ Deployed first successful imaging and associated system in company history. Within 4 years, 3,000+ employees had access to this system; employees using parts of it had increased productivity of 45%+. By the end of 2001, more than 150M imaging pages were stored and available.
➤ Led team of internal and external resources that built out 158 branch locations in 3 years.
➤ Led team that worked with 4 different vendors to deploy one of the first POS device applications across 3 different platforms in the industry. 4M+ applications ultimately processed via these devices.
➤ Led combined internal and external team that converted 9 different loan portfolios (8 credit card, 1 mortgage) in a span of 24 months.
➤ Deployed to 76 branches (1,500+ FTE) a mortgage loan origination system that originated more than $4B in loans by 1999. Project duration from contract signing to final branch deployment was 1 year and 1 week. Ultimately, 158 branches used this system to originate loans. Total project cost was $4.5M. Featured in Progress Software's publication for IT application project.
➤ Deployed the first Voice Response Unit. Grew from a 1-division, 48-port system to a 5-division, 336-port system processing 750,000 calls/month, with 9 distinct, functional applications.

HOME INTERNATIONAL—Edina, MN   1988–1995
A diversified provider of consumer lending products.

AVP–BUSINESS OPERATIONS MANAGER
Started as an internal operations auditor. After 15 months, moved to the core business operations of the private-label credit card division of Home International (Home Retail Services Inc.). Managed 80+ staff.

HANSON, ASHLEY & LARSON, Public Accounting Auditor—Mendota, MN   1986–1988

PROFESSIONAL TRAINING, EDUCATION & CERTIFICATION

Asset & Liability Management, Sponsored by Home Retail, 40 hours, 1994
Six Sigma Greenbelt training, Sponsored by MFA, 40 hours, 2004

B.S., Accounting—Northeastern University, Boston, MA

Certified Public Accountant

Resume Transformation #17: Tabitha Harris

Resume Writer:

> Marjorie Sussman, MRW, CPRW
> 411 Washington Ave.
> Cliffside Park, NJ 07010
> Phone: (201) 942-8237
> E-mail: marjorie1130@aol.com

The Situation

About to leave the Air Force after 10 years, Tabitha was interested in pursuing a position as a human resources or training manager. Because most of her experience had been in technical operations, she was stumped as to how to present her experiences to position her for her dream jobs.

The "Before" Version

Tabitha's resume is overly long (five pages) and crammed full of precisely the things she does not want to do in her next job.

The "After" Version—Applying the Five Resume Makeover Strategies

- **Fashion a Strong Framework.** Although a functional resume would make sense to help Tabitha transition to a new field, the chronological format also works well—as long as it focuses on her human resources and training activities and not her systems analysis and project management roles.

- **Start with a Superlative Summary.** Beginning with the headline and proceeding through five relevant bullet points, Tabitha's summary clearly positions her for her target jobs.

- **Emphasize Experience and Accomplishments.** Relevant activities and accomplishments are presented in an easy-to-read format. Because the resume is so much more concise, each of the bullet points stands out as a meaningful accomplishment.

- **Enhance with Education and "Extras."** Tabitha's extensive list of technical training has been eliminated, and now just her degrees and her commendations make up the final section of her resume.

- **Proofread and Polish to Perfection.** Although it's not fancy, Tabitha's new format is classic, clean, and easy to read.

TABITHA HARRIS
411 Sixteenth Street ♦ Des Moines, Iowa 55555
Daytime/Evening: 555-367-5555 ♦ E-mail: tabitha@aol.com
CLEARANCE: Held a Secret clearance until September 8, 2005; good until August 2007

Over eight years of extensive qualifications experience in information management, information assurance, and resource programs as well as audio and video communication systems. Results-oriented professional with expertise in planning, development, and delivery of technology and communication solutions to meet challenging business demands.

SUMMARY OF QUALIFICATIONS

Information Systems Management	Hardware/Software Skills	Training/Supervision
Policy/Procedure Development	Database Management	Resource Management
Organizational Development	Customer Focus/Team Building	Time Management

PROFESSIONAL EXPERIENCE

Data Management Systems Analyst
Plans and Programs, Hanscom Air Force Base, Massachusetts   2005-Present
Provide data and administrative management support to Air Force top management; implement a Balanced Scorecard (BSC) metric collection systems; establish a baseline of hardware, software, documentation, processes, and collection system requirements necessary to implement BSC reporting tools; continued to evaluate possible use of other existing commercial-off-the-shelf software and future Air Force systems for data extraction processes, analysis methodology and reporting requirements; leveraged existing and future systems to the maximum extent and reduce investment costs; train, and publicize strategy implementation across the base.
- Conducted analysis of several metric collection systems and after careful evaluation of capabilities of each, recommended implementation of Strategic Management of Information Systems (SMIS) Reporting tool—in less than one month; SMIS offered the following advantages to government: automation, successfully implemented at other Air Force (AF) organizations, user-friendly, accessible through AF Portal, offers multiple capabilities (collection, data repository, trend analysis, roll-up or drill-down capability, etc.) and will interface with other existing AF systems; can be implemented quickly; is cost-effective (e.g. no new development required; changes/mods paid for by higher headquarters); and can be tailored/adapted to meet Electronic Systems Center needs.
- Implement and leverage SMIS to store, automate and standardize metric data across the base; coordinated with base information assurance and network team to set up accounts for 20+ users to easily access SMIS application via online; provide technical support to include modifications to adapt the system to future changing requirements
- Develop, execute, and enforce metric data collection and reporting processes and procedures by implementing, managing and monitoring monthly reporting suspense tracking systems; analyze data, develop documentation and train 20+ users on the use of the data management system
- Analyze, monitor, and interpret measurement data to include evaluating and preparing recommendations on data trends and new issues to top management
- Ensure the currency, accuracy, and integrity of the data management system; utilize its knowledge, the BSC process, metrics, and customer requirements; ensure that data is reported in a timely and accurate manner; provide technical and management review of progress to the government on a monthly basis

Figure 4.33: Before.   *(continued)*

(continued)

Tabitha Harris

- Manage and implement BSC and Air Force Smart Operations of 21-Century (AFSO21)/Lean initiatives marketing campaign
- Assist in generating newspaper articles, online newsletters, and e-mail marketing campaigns; develop, design (using Adobe Photoshop Creative Suite and Xara applications), and print over 100 display panels and 500+ brochures for advertising and promulgating information dissemination in eight high traffic areas within two months--ensure base community BSC information awareness and top management's decision-making process
- Organize and prepare working papers, presentation slides, and documentation for meetings to assist with decision-making, and policies; support the preparation and development of reports, working papers, and producing documentation at all management levels
- Designed, developed, and managed BSC web page for organization using FrontPage; ensured personnel across the base including three geographically separated locations has easy access to information and resources
    - Reconstruct, streamline, and manage file folders, documents, and links; organized content for easier navigation and user-friendly

Information Technology Specialist
Electronic Systems Center (ESC), Hanscom Air Force Base, Massachusetts   *2003-2005*
Personally handpicked for the position because of ability to deal effectively and professionally with different levels of management, and external personnel including vendors, DoD industries, and contractors. Responsible for planning, coordinating, and facilitating over 500 plus audio and video teleconferences to high level staff offices critical to world-wide decision making. Supervised the activities of two subordinates and responsible for additional duties including managing the Intranet web page, computer equipment database, training, and supply inventory control, and telecommunications.

- Managed and administered records program for directorate staff division; created, designed, and implemented all new comprehensive file plans consisting of records in both paper form as well as electronic versions on shared network, electronic media, and Intranet webpage; ensured all file plans was easily accessible, and user-friendly.
    - Ensured sections have appointed records custodians; trained custodians on the use of Records Management software; worked with each section to streamline outdated file plan; applied file cutoff procedures, and disposed records according to records disposition instructions in preparation of base annual inspection.
    - Conducted quarterly self-inspections to ensure 100 percent compliance with disposition; resulted in an "Outstanding" rating during the annual Base Staff Assistance Visit inspection.
- Managed and redesigned Intranet web page for distribution of information resources; providing immediate access to executive-level management tools for all base personnel.
- Developed and managed computer equipment database for over 200 computer systems valued at $450,000; simplified tracking, reconciled over $5,000 in errors, and ensured 100 percent accountability.
- Administered computer security and information assurance program to 40+ personnel; ensured users are trained and updated on DOD directives and local policies, resulting in zero vulnerabilities leading to ESC's 99 percent performance rating for the Air Force Material Command.
- Utilized Polycom, PictureTel, and Tandberg audio/video communication systems to plan, coordinate, execute over 500 audio and video teleconferences to high level staff offices resulting in efficient operations critical to world-wide decision-making processes.
    - Handpicked by senior leadership to provide information technology support, and coordinated facilitation for Congressional Staffers' visit; ensured flawless execution

Tabitha Harris

- Coordinated and executed over 500 briefings for Air Force flag-level staffs (foreign and domestic), Pentagon Secretary of Acquisition, Program Executive Office in execution of a $5.4B, 150 plus program, Information Technology portfolio, and seven geographically separated locations
- Coordinated with vendor and government contractor to upgrade command staff's conference room for Defense Video Services-Global certification in only one week; ensured minimal disruption to critical video teleconference schedule involving top management and higher headquarters—one-third upgrade time
- Developed comprehensive operating instructions on how to operate the two audio/video communication systems in two conference rooms; ensure basic understanding of facilitating audio/video teleconferences

Information Manager, Staff Support
Command/Control Enterprise Integration Office, Hanscom Air Force Base, Massachusetts   2001–2003
Handpicked by directorate to manage flow and life cycle of information through manual and automated technology to include maintaining, planning, and controlling programs, policies, and procedures concerning office systems, records, administrative communications, and unit mail procedures; managed budget, information systems and computer resources.

- Accomplished periodic assessment and revision as required of directorate policies, procedures and goal performance; identified process improvement alternatives for office product quality and efficiency; reduced processing time by 20 %
- Established new file system for seven divisions; reorganized and consolidated file plans into one; defined local requirements, and ensured documents were created, maintained and destroyed in accordance with disposition instructions, and DoD directives.
  - Assisted with unit Intranet web page implementation plan; moved program files to collaborative environment; identified files for deletion, organized storage space, and established file standards for seven divisions; reduced volume on network drive by 50 percent.
- Co-developed and standardized Oracle web-based suspense tracking systems for performance reports and awards programs
  - Ensured seven separate divisions received accurate weekly suspenses; worked with base personnel office to ensure the divisions received monthly up-to-date military and civilian rosters.
  - Identified future performance reports and award packages ahead of schedule enabling supervisors to prepare timely reports in a very high "tempo" environment--resulted in 100 percent on-time submission rate.
- Managed and performed administrative quality control checks on all military and civilian performance reports, award packages, and correspondences
  - Established new processes and procedures for better quality control; reduced volume by 50 percent.
  - Researched, analyzed, organized, and developed PowerPoint presentation for and trained over 50 personnel on performance reports and awards program; improved completion rate by 16 percent.
- Streamlined copier service replacement process; conducted cost-benefit analysis; resulted in $8,200 savings.
- Managed and administered supply budget procedures for 340 employees; revamped ordering process; tracked crucial computer resources and office supplies purchases; resulting in 100 percent accountability; reduced budget spending by 10 percent through aggressive identification of efficiencies.
- Established telephone service requests with Defense Metropolitan Area Telephone Systems team; researched and verified validity of calls from telephone billing statements; corrected discrepancies on the spot; ensured cost effective utilization of government funds and equipment; identified 130

(continued)

(continued)

Tabitha Harris

unused telephone numbers within three separate facilities on base; saved unit $30,000 in program funds.

Information Management Specialist, Staff Support
45 Contracting Squadron, Patrick Air Force Base, Florida   2000–2001
611 Air Support Squadron, Elmendorf Air Force Base, Alaska   1997-2000

- Administered Records Information Management Systems software on user desktops; conducted a one-on-one training to five administrators on the use of software, and managing records; reduced data entry by 20 percent.
- Managed $125 million operations and maintenance service contracts for Alaskan radar sites; resulted in timely disposition and archiving contracts.
- Processed and administered administrative orders, arranged travel, accommodations, and local transportation for 18 flight members—guaranteed flight members' travel to 21 geographically separated sites in remote Alaska.
- Managed and developed automated suspense tracking system on Microsoft Access database for correspondences, award packages, performance reports, and staff packages
  - Created new internal coordination document to organize and track incoming and outgoing packages; established new processes on how suspenses were to be coordinated to command section; attention to detail resulted in maintaining late suspense status to zero percent.
- Managed unit's activity distribution office mail; dispersed all incoming and outgoing official mail; processed and distributed over 3,000 pieces of official mail; tracked and distributed over 200 accountable and classified packages with zero security violations.
- Developed and managed processes and procedures for four government vehicles; trained personnel about maintaining, servicing, and safely driving—ensured safety and zero violations.
- Analyzed and researched security issues; briefed and trained personnel on communication, computer, emission, and operation security, and antiterrorism awareness—resulted in zero security violations.
- Coordinated telephone work order requests with Civil Engineering team during unit reorganization; expedited work orders to activate 130 phones, voicemails, and four fax machines—ensured minimal disruptions to workflow.
- Planned, coordinated, and executed all official office functions and events including reserving locations, schedules, and programs—guaranteed smooth operation.
- Created and managed unit quarterly and annually awards program; provided recognition to all outstanding performers—fostered team environment and boost morale.
- Managed and operated office information systems (stand alone and network) to create, collect, use, access, disseminate, maintain, and dispose of information; set up computer links to key mission data to include staff meeting presentation slides, computer security training, unit's organization structure through Intranet web page.
- Provided assistance to network users on hardware/software configuration problems; recommended preventive actions to customers to preclude recurring hardware/software problems or system inefficiencies.
- Maintained server by using administrative tools such as backing up data information, cleaning out event logs, and windows diagnostics; accomplish new and recurring software installation and records maintenance requirements necessary to keep current with technology—implemented AF and Department of Defense (DOD) policies and instructions about use of government computers.
-

EDUCATION/TRAINING

WESTERN NEW ENGLAND COLLEGE, SPRINGFIELD, MASSACHUSETTS
Enrolled in M.S., Engineering Management, completed 9 semester hours.

Tabitha Harris

WESTERN NEW ENGLAND COLLEGE, SPRINGFIELD, MASSACHUSETTS
B.S., Business Administration, Computer Information Systems, *Summa Cum Laude*, 2004.

COMMUNITY COLLEGE OF THE AIR FORCE
A.A.S., Information Resource Management, 2002

Records Management
Quality Management
Balanced Scorecard Training
Client Systems Management Certification
Operation Security/Information Assurance
Information Security/Information Systems Security

ADDITIONAL SKILLS

- Proficient in Microsoft Office applications: PowerPoint, Access, Excel, Word, FrontPage, Publisher, Outlook
- Understand fundamentals and concepts of networking, systems design and analysis, data communications, information systems, systems engineering, Adobe Photoshop Creative Suite 2, Xara, Balanced Scorecard, and Six Sigma
- Exceptional interpersonal skills with a talent for analyzing problems, developing and simplifying procedures, and finding innovative solutions
- Excellent verbal and written communicator

TABITHA HARRIS

411 Sixteenth Street • Des Moines, Iowa 55555
555-367-5555 • tabitha@aol.com

HUMAN RESOURCES / TRAINING MANAGER

World-class professional with 10 years of experience working successfully with all levels of personnel in time-critical settings. Provide unique balance of technical savvy and strong personal and professional relationships.

➢ **Provided key leadership in transitioning workforce** to new computer systems and lean initiatives through individualized and online training, preparation of guideline manuals, and e-learning resources.

➢ **Recruited, trained, and mentored** electronic records custodians to ensure accuracy of information, timely delivery, and adherence to regulatory guidelines.

➢ **Prepared and delivered internal and external communications** to publicize awareness of new security and information distribution measures.

➢ **Developed and standardized Oracle Web-based tracking system for performance reports and awards** programs that guaranteed 100% on-time and accurate submission rate.

➢ **Demonstrated strong computer skills** in Microsoft Office (Word, Excel, PowerPoint, Access, Outlook), FrontPage, and Publisher; Adobe Photoshop; and Creative Suite 2.

Budget Administration | Staff Management | Policy Development | Professional Communications |
Confidential Information Management | Training & Support | Interdepartmental Liaison & Partnerships

PROFESSIONAL EXPERIENCE

UNITED STATES AIR FORCE   1997–Present
DATA MANAGEMENT SYSTEMS ANALYST / PLANS AND PROGRAMS, 2006–Present

Provide administrative and data support to top management. Develop, monitor, and enforce metric data collection and reporting procedures based on suspense tracking systems. Compile and prepare working papers, presentations, and documentation for senior staff decision-making meetings. Collaborate with cross-functional teams to set up data management systems accounts and train new users. Analyze and interpret measurement data to recommend system improvements.

Key Achievements:

▪ **Spearheaded efforts to transition workforce** to Balanced Scorecard (BSC) and Smart Operations of the 21st Century through one-on-one and online training, preparation of storyboards, brochures, quick reference guides, and newsletters and the implementation of a dedicated Web page and e-publication resources.

▪ **Authored communications** that effectively marketed awareness of BSC and Smart Operations and significantly quickened adoption of the new systems.

▪ **Implemented BSC metric collection system,** establishing hardware, software, documentation, and collection system requirements to support reporting tools.

INFORMATION TECHNOLOGY SPECIALIST / ELECTRONIC SYSTEMS CENTER, 2003–2006

Tapped for this position based on proven ability to communicate effectively with all levels of management and third-party vendors. Coordinated logistics of and facilitated more than 500 audio/video teleconferences to high-level staff offices critical to worldwide decision-making. Supervised two-member staff and managed intranet Web page, computer equipment database, training, supply inventory control, and telecommunications.

Key Achievements:

▪ **Commended for excellence in managing and administering records program,** creating and implementing comprehensive paper and electronic files on user-friendly shared network.

Figure 4.34: After.

TABITHA HARRIS

555-367-5555 • tabitha@aol.com

- **Appointed, trained, and monitored records custodians** to ensure compliance with official guidelines.
- **Developed operating instruction manuals and trained personnel** on communications systems and teleconferencing.
- **Redesigned intranet site for distribution of information resources,** providing immediate access to executive-level management tools for all personnel.
- **Provided training to more than 40 staff members** on new computer security and information assurance policies, resulting in zero vulnerabilities and 99% performance rating.
- **Developed computer equipment database** for computer systems, simplified tracking, reconciled more than $5K in errors, and ensured 100% accountability.

INFORMATION MANAGER, STAFF SUPPORT / ENTERPRISE INTEGRATION OFFICE, 2001–2003

Chosen by directors to manage flow and life cycle of information through manual and automated technology. Planned, monitored, and maintained programs, policies, and procedures governing office systems, records, administrative communications, and mail. Administered IS budget and managed computer resources.

Key Achievements:

- **Consolidated file system for 7 divisions** into a single streamlined system.
- **Assisted with intranet Web page implementation,** moving and deleting files, organizing storage space, and establishing file standards.
- **Developed and standardized Oracle Web-based tracking system for performance reports and awards programs** to ensure 100% on-time submission rate.
- **Managed accuracy of all performance reports, award packages,** and correspondence.
- **Instituted time- and cost-saving initiatives** with copier service, supplies vendor, and telephone service.

INFORMATION MANAGEMENT SPECIALIST, 1997–2001

Oversaw and administered Records Information Management Systems software training. Identified and resolved hardware and software issues. Managed $125M in operations and maintenance service contracts.

Key Achievements:

- **Designed/developed automated suspense tracking system** that secured 100% on-time submissions.
- **Assisted Y2K crisis management team** by setting up instant messaging service to enable real-time communications among geographically distant teams.

EDUCATION & RECOGNITIONS

WESTERN NEW ENGLAND COLLEGE, Springfield, MA
M.S. in Engineering Management
B.S. in Business Administration/Computer Information Systems, *Summa cum Laude*—2004

Recipient of many awards, including *Outstanding Information Manager, Outstanding Airman,* and
Outstanding Noncommissioned Officer

Resume Transformation #18: Derek D'Angelo

Resume Writer:

Louise Kursmark, MRW, CPRW, JCTC, CEIP, CCM
Best Impression Career Services, Inc.
24 White Oaks Lane
Reading, MA 01867
Phone: (781) 944-2471
E-mail: LK@yourbestimpression.com
www.yourbestimpression.com
www.resumewritingacademy.com

The Situation

Derek's true love was building successful biotechnology companies. Currently in a role of commercializing technology for a medical college, he was eager to return to a corporate setting. He was concerned that his current position in academia would be a strike against him.

The "Before" Version

Derek had created a straightforward chronological resume beginning with an Objective statement. In his desire not to overwhelm readers with his extensive experience, he had shortchanged himself by not appropriately highlighting all of his impressive achievements. Plus, Derek included dates back to 1965, advertising his age at well above 60.

The "After" Version—Applying the Five Resume Makeover Strategies

- **Fashion a Strong Framework.** Primarily chronological, the "after" resume condenses several of Derek's consulting experiences into one section and severely contracts the details of his academic background. This enabled the resume to remain on two pages while allowing for the addition of much relevant detail about his experiences and accomplishments.

- **Start with a Superlative Summary.** Derek's Summary is crisp and concise. It uses a headline and subheadings to identify his expertise and then three short paragraphs to describe his qualifications as a senior executive, an expert in building viable biotech companies, and an effective leader. A keywords section, titled "Areas of Expertise," is

154

followed by Derek's "wow" achievements—a "Career Highlights" section of six specific, quantified results he achieved while leading biotech organizations.

- **Emphasize Experience and Accomplishments.** A strong opening sentence describes the context, challenge, and key accomplishment of each of Derek's positions. Other position details are briefly stated, and several strong accomplishment statements are included for each position.

- **Enhance with Education and "Extras."** Derek's educational qualifications are extremely important, but putting "Ph.D." after his name on the very first line of the resume immediately places him in an academic environment. Instead, this impressive credential is moved to the Education section, which also includes brief summaries of his research and teaching background.

- **Proofread and Polish to Perfection.** Although quite text-heavy, Derek's resume is easy to skim because it is well organized and most paragraphs and bullet points are just two or three lines long. This required extensive editing, rewriting, and review of the material to be sure everything included was relevant and important.

Derek D'Angelo, Ph.D.

1004 Footbridge Trail, San Antonio, TX 78215
830–459–0014
ddangelo@gmail.com

Objective:
Return to corporate environment as a
BIOTECH EXECUTIVE

BUSINESS EXPERIENCE & ACHIEVEMENTS

DATONAH MEDICAL COLLEGE, Datonah, TX   2006-Present
Director of Technology Transfer & Economic Development
- Manage the College's intellectual property, patenting and licensing
- Assist in Economic Development through the formation of new local business ventures

DEWEY BOND & TRAFALGAR, CONSULTANTS, Atlanta, GA   2005
Principal Consultant
- Assisted in growing the firm's life science client base in Eastern U.S.

BIOSCIENCES RESEARCH AND COMMERCIALIZATION CENTER, Columbus, GA   2004-2005
Executive Director
- Worked with local business leaders to attract new biotechnology companies to Southeast U.S.
- Provided start-up assistance to new life science companies

BIOCELL, INC., Raleigh, NC   1999-2004
President & Chief Executive Officer
- Co-founder of this cell-therapy device manufacturing firm
- In-licensed the company's proprietary cell-delivery device technology
- Financed the start-up operations with $2 million in private investment capital
- Established a broad collaborative partnership with a worldwide pharmaceutical company
- Developed clinical research collaborations with over 30 academic and industry R&D groups

BAKER HEALTHCARE CORPORATION, Raleigh, NC   1993-1999
Vice President of Business Development, Immunotherapy Division
- Managed the business development, strategic planning and corporate communication functions
- Acquired proprietary therapeutic cytokines for use in ex vivo cancer treatment protocols
- Divested the Division's autoimmune therapy system to a European investor group
- Formed a national network of Cell Processing Partnerships in order to accelerate market acceptance of the company's new stem cell purification system

INDEPENDENT CONSULTANT, Raleigh, NC   1989-1993
Principal
- Acquired $1 million in seed capital to start a new drug-delivery company
- Created a cancer therapy collaboration between a monoclonal antibody company and a manufacturer of chemotherapeutic agents
- Provided technology evaluation services to local agencies including the State University

Figure 4.35: Before.

BIO SCIENCE SAFETY, INC., Research Triangle Park, NC   1987-1989
President & Chief Executive Officer
- Co-founder of this pharmaceutical bio-safety testing laboratory
- Licensed proprietary virus technology for company's initial service offerings
- Obtained $2.4 million in venture capital to begin company operations
- Managed laboratory operations and sales to achieve first-year revenue of $1 million

BIODIAGNOSTICS, INC., Research Triangle Park, NC   1984-1987
Vice President of Applied Science / Business Manager, In Vitro Diagnostics
- Acquired proprietary biopharmaceuticals for two limited R&D financial partnerships
- General Manager of the Diagnostic Business Unit; achieved annual sales growth of 25% three years running

HARRIS BIOMEDICAL, INC., Research Triangle Park, NC   1983-1984
Vice President of Research & Development
- Developed a five-year strategic plan for the company's R&D investment
- Recruited a staff of senior scientists in diagnostics, blood banking and instrumentation

MIDWEST LABORATORIES—Diagnostic Division, Chicago, IL   1977-1983
Director of Research & Development
- Led a team of 60 scientists in developing 15 highly successful tests to detect blood-borne pathogens, infectious agents and cancer
- Delivered timely marketing, regulatory and field support for the Division's sales force
- Managed reagent manufacturing for the Cancer business unit to achieve rapid market penetration

TEACHING APPOINTMENTS

UNIVERSITY OF ILLINOIS   1976-1977
Assistant Professor of Oral Biology

SPRINGFIELD COLLEGE   1971-1976
Assistant Professor of Chemistry

EDUCATION & RESEARCH

SPRINGFIELD COLLEGE   1970-1971
Research Associate, Department of Oral Biology

BIO-SCIENCES, INC.   1969-1970
Senior Scientist, Central Research Laboratories

UNIVERSITY OF CHICAGO   1969
PhD, Biochemistry

UNIVERSITY OF ILLINOIS   1965
BA, Chemistry

Derek D'Angelo

830-459-0014 • ddangelo@gmail.com
1004 Footbridge Trail, San Antonio, TX 78215

Senior Executive

BIOTECHNOLOGY / MEDICAL DEVICES / BIOPHARMACEUTICALS / DIAGNOSTICS

Business development and operations executive, expert in identifying, developing, and commercializing high-value medical products, services, and innovative business initiatives.

Catalyst for translating scientific innovations into profitable technologies and products—leading successful start-ups, driving technology transfer and licensing deals, developing a strategic sales portfolio, and forging alliances with venture investors, technical innovators, and established medical and pharmaceutical companies.

Inspirational leader able to communicate company strategy, performance, and promise to customers, partners, future investors, and current stakeholders.

AREAS OF EXPERTISE

- Vision & Strategic Planning
- P&L Management
- Fund-raising & VC Relationships
- Strategic Mergers & Alliances
- Deal Structure & Negotiation

- In & Out Licensing
- Pharmaceutical Contract Services
- Entrepreneurial Start-up / New Product Launch
- Intellectual Property Evaluation & Management
- Product Development Cycle Timing & Management

CAREER HIGHLIGHTS

- Led BioCell from start-up to $2M capital-raising and collaboration with European pharmaceutical giant.
- Co-founded biotech services company Bio Science Safety and generated $1M in first-year revenue.
- Identified buyer and executed divestiture of Baker's $200M Immunotherapy Division to RX Corporation.
- Spurred 40% increase in medical-research patent filings in 1 year for a medical research institution.
- Generated 25% annual sales growth in Biodiagnostics's In Vitro Business Unit for 3 straight years.
- Drove development of 15 medical diagnostic tests that generated $500M sales in first 3 years for Midwest Labs.

Experience and Achievements

Director of Technology Transfer and Economic Development, 2006–Present
DATONAH MEDICAL COLLEGE, Datonah, TX

Brought on board to invigorate and manage the patenting and commercialization of therapies, compounds, and devices emerging from leading-edge research performed at medical and dental schools—only recently transitioned to research institution. Built credibility and trust with faculty and successfully educated on the need to patent as well as publish. Manage full scope of intellectual property for the college. Direct legal, scientific, and marketing staff.

- Evaluated 62 Invention Disclosures and advanced 37 to patent application (+40% over prior year) in areas of gene therapy, biopharmaceuticals, medicinal compounds, and medical devices.
- Cultivated a pipeline of new patent applications by instituting early-stage meetings with senior scientists.
- Promoted technology-transfer capabilities at trade shows and enticed (to date) 1 regenerative medicine start-up to relocate to Datonah.

President and Chief Executive Officer, 1999–2004 • **Board Member,** 1999–Present
BIOCELL, INC., Raleigh, NC

Led biopharmaceutical start-up through capital raising, technology development, and alliance with major European pharmaceutical company. Negotiated in-licensing of technology portfolio from Baker Healthcare; assembled scientific and business team; brought company from concept to operation in 6 months. Managed P&L, operations, and business development; provided market-focused guidance to team developing cell-delivery device technology.

- Raised $2M in private investment capital.
- Developed clinical research collaborations with 30+ academic and industry R&D groups.
- Initiated relationship with State University for innovative use of drug-delivery system for multiple sclerosis.

Figure 4.36: After.

Derek D'Angelo   830-459-0014 • ddangelo@gmail.com

BIOCELL, INC., continued

- Negotiated out-licensing deal and established broad collaborative partnership with Franke Munich, an $11B German pharmaceutical company; managed the relationship over 4+ years during development of an innovative immunosuppressive cell therapy system for use in diabetes treatment.
- Identified several candidates to acquire the company and infuse new capital; currently in discussions.

Business Development Consultant, 2004–2006 and 1989–1993

Provided technology commercialization / life sciences expertise to help public- and private-sector organizations achieve strategic business objectives. Highlights include:

- Grew executive recruiting firm Dewey Bond & Trafalgar life science client base in Eastern U.S. through aggressive business development with technology and biotech companies from start-ups to Fortune 1000.
- Attracted biotechnology companies to Southeast U.S. for Biosciences Research & Commercialization Center.
- Acquired $1M in seed capital to launch a new drug-delivery company.
- Created collaboration between a monoclonal antibody company and a manufacturer of chemotherapeutic agents.

Vice President of Business Development, 1993–1999

BAKER HEALTHCARE CORPORATION—Immunotherapy Division, Raleigh, NC

Recruited to identify partners and markets for new immunotherapy technology. Managed business development, strategic planning, and corporate communications functions for $200M division of $10B industry leader in medical equipment, supplies, and therapies.

- Orchestrated 10 in-licensing deals, acquiring therapeutic cytokines and antibodies for *ex vivo* cancer protocols.
- Divested the division's autoimmune therapy system to a European investor group for $15M.
- Accelerated market acceptance of new stem-cell purification system by forming a national network of cell-processing partnerships.
- Licensed Oncopross, a new blood processor for the treatment of cancer, to Columbia Oncology, Inc.
- Formed marketing alliance with Dana Cancer Institute.

President and Chief Executive Officer, 1987–1989

BIO SCIENCE SAFETY, INC., Research Triangle Park, NC

Co-founded pharmaceutical bio-safety testing laboratory and led from start-up to $1M in first-year revenue. Worked with 2 VC investment groups on company launch and strategic direction. Managed lab operations and sales.

- Secured $2.4M in venture capital to support business launch.
- Licensed proprietary virus technology for company's initial service offerings.
- Generated rapid revenue ($1M+), leading to investor split and new company direction.

Vice President of Applied Science / Business Manager, In Vitro Diagnostics, 1984–1987

BIODIAGNOSTICS, INC., Research Triangle Park, NC

Acquired proprietary biopharmaceuticals for 2 limited R&D partnerships and grew sales 25% per year 3 years running for the Diagnostic Business Unit. Managed team of 25 and distribution operations in the US, Europe, and Japan.

Prior Professional Experience

- **VP Research & Development,** Harris BioMedical: Created 5-year strategic plan for company's R&D investment.
- **Director of R&D,** Midwest Laboratories: Led a team of 60 scientists in developing 15 highly successful tests to detect blood-borne pathogens, infectious agents, and cancer; achieved combined sales of $500M in first 3 years.

Professional Profile

Education	PhD, Biochemistry, University of Chicago • BA, Chemistry, University of Illinois
Teaching	University of Illinois (Oral Biology); Springfield College (Chemistry)
Research	Springfield College (Oral Biology); Bio-Sciences, Inc. (Central Research Laboratories)

Before moving on to your cover letter and the rest of your job search, compare your new resume to the "after" samples in this chapter. While each resume is unique (and yours should be, too), they have in common a sharp focus, achievement orientation, and strategic approach to supporting each job-seeker's objectives.

Should you decide to work with a professional resume writer, start by contacting the writers featured in this book, using their work samples as part of your decision-making process. They can help you transform your "before" resume to a shining "after" example.

Key Points: Chapter 4

- Use the Five Resume Makeover Strategies to transform your resume from a "before" to an outstanding "after":

  1. Fashion a Strong Framework
  2. Start with a Superlative Summary
  3. Emphasize Experience and Accomplishments
  4. Enhance with Education and "Extras"
  5. Proofread and Polish to Perfection

- Compare your resume to the before-and-after examples to get new ideas for design, language, formatting, and positioning.

Chapter 5

Create a Killer Cover Letter

Because cover letters are such an important part of your job search, I didn't want to omit them from this book. However, the topic is extensive—in fact, I have written two complete books on cover letters! Much of the advice in this brief chapter is excerpted from my companion book in the "Help in a Hurry" series—*15-Minute Cover Letter.* I encourage you to pick up that book or the more in-depth *Cover Letter Magic* if you'd like additional ideas and assistance with your cover letters.

Cover Letter Basics

First, understand that you will need some kind of covering note with every resume you send—whether filling out an online application, e-mailing your resume in response to a job ad, reaching out to your network, following up on a referral, or cold-calling potential employers. All of these communications can be called "cover letters," but obviously you would write a much different note to a close friend or a business colleague than you would to an employer whose name you don't even know.

The purpose of cover letters is to tell your recipients what they're receiving and why. A good cover letter is a valuable adjunct to your resume and helps to convince your readers of your capabilities. What you say and how you say it should be a continuation of the messages you created for your resume.

Let's examine each of the different circumstances when you'll be sending letters and discuss the details of each and the differences between them. Then I'll provide a brief three-step plan for creating relevant and meaningful content for all of your cover letters.

Transmission Guidelines

- When completing online applications, look for a separate box where you can type or paste your cover letter.

- When sending a resume by e-mail, write your cover letter in the body of the e-mail and attach your resume as a Word document.

- Should you decide to print and mail your resume, print your cover letter on matching paper and use the same stationery heading with your name and contact information. Center your letter on the page and sign the original using a good, dark pen.

Tone, Style, and Content Guidelines

- Any letters to people you don't know, including e-mail letters applying to posted openings, are considered formal business correspondence. Begin with a formal salutation—"Dear Mr. (Last Name)" or "Dear Ms. (Last Name)"—and close with "Sincerely" and your typed name.

- When writing e-mails, keep your letter as crisp as possible. You want to capture the reader's attention in the few lines of text that are available on the screen even if it's a BlackBerry or other handheld device for reading e-mail.

- Your printed and mailed letters can be a bit longer, but keep them readable with short paragraphs, and don't overload your readers with non-essential information.

- For e-mails to friends and colleagues, you can use a less formal tone than you would for a business letter to a stranger. However, don't get sloppy—use correct language, not text-message shortcuts, and be sure to spell-check.

Three Steps to a Great Cover Letter

Follow these steps and you'll create an effective letter in no time.

Step 1: State Why You're Writing

The first paragraph of your letter should let your reader know why you are writing. Have you been referred by a mutual acquaintance? Are you following up on a phone or e-mail message? Are you applying for an advertised position? Don't be mysterious! Share this information up front so that your reader can place your letter in the proper context.

Try to make your opening sentence interesting enough to draw the reader in to the rest of your letter. We don't suggest that you get too clever or "gimmicky," but do avoid dry, overused introductions such as "I am writing to inquire about positions with your company." Instead, write something that will make your reader want to know more about you and how you can help with a specific problem or challenge. Here are a few ideas for doing that:

- **Drop a name:** "Chris Wilkins suggested that I contact you to see if my supply chain expertise and record of accomplishments with XYZ Industries would be of interest to you at Worldwide."

- **Lead with a "wow" achievement:** "Under my leadership as Sales & Marketing VP for MoneyMakers, we grew market share from 10% to 24% on a shoestring budget. I'd like to speak with you about opportunities where I can deliver this level of sales results for Acme Funds."

- **Reference the specific opportunity:** "Your need for an Accounting Manager who can lead cost-cutting efforts caught my attention. At Carlyle Company, my greatest achievements have been in the areas of operational streamlining and expense reduction."

- **Quote a relevant article:** "I was interested to read in *Business Monthly* that San Marcos plans to expand its Asian operations to Vietnam and China. With seven years of experience launching production (both plant start-up and supplier development) in both of these countries, I can help make this important venture successful for you."

- **Quote a recent industry statistic:** "Healthcare workers are in the shortest supply since the 1950s, according to a recent article in *Health Careers*. If you are experiencing this shortage at County General, I believe you will be interested in my qualifications as a surgical technician and my strong desire to join your team."

- **Quote your contact directly:** "'Companies succeed by hiring the right people—people who want to make a difference, not just do a job.' When I read this statement in your interview that was recently published in the *Chicago Tribune*, I knew that General Widget was a great fit for my energy and passion as well as my skills as a machinist."

In this opening paragraph, try to communicate one or two relevant facts about yourself that will be of interest to your reader. Employers are not interested in your life story or even your complete career history at this point. They want to know, "Why are you contacting me and why should I care?" Open your letter on a strong note by answering these questions.

Step 2: Share Information Relevant to the Reader's Needs

Here is the heart of your letter: the middle paragraph or two, or the brief list of bullet points, that tells the reader something about you that is relevant to his or her needs.

If you're responding to a job posting, you can pull out pertinent details and address them in your cover letter, as seen in the following two examples:

Customer Service Associate

If you love talking with people, solving problems, and working with prestigious clients, this position is for you. You will assist employees from a growing client list with questions about their benefit plans and help them solve complex issues related to their health, savings, and retirement plans.

You will have an opportunity to use your
— Excellent communication skills
— Computer knowledge
— Analytical skills
— Problem-solving capabilities

Minimum requirements include
— A stable work history
— At least two years of continuous customer service experience
— Knowledge of Windows and Internet

My experience in the fast-paced environment of a technical call center is directly relevant to your needs. For the past three years, I have helped employees from all departments and all locations of our global company resolve various technical problems. This requires not only excellent technical skills, but patience, attentive listening, and the ability to explain technical solutions to non-technical workers. My efforts have been so successful, I have twice earned "Customer Service Rep of the Quarter" from among more than 300 people at our call center.

Note how this brief paragraph addresses the key requirements of the position and also provides evidence of this candidate's ability to do the job well.

Here is another example.

Transportation Manager: Excellent career opportunity! Individual will be responsible for implementing and developing cost-saving programs, in addition to improving load efficiencies and transportation processes.

Requirements:
**3–5 years transportation supervisory experience
**3–5 years transportation industry experience servicing large retail accounts
**10 years domestic transportation (Rail, LTL, TL carriers)
**Working knowledge of U.S. Transportation regulations and comfortable with transportation practices in all U.S. regions
**Documented success of improving cost and efficiencies of transportation operations

Educational Requirement:
**Bachelor's degree in Transportation, Logistics, or Business

Computer Knowledge:
**Proficient with MS Office
** Transportation Management Software

Interpersonal Skills:
**Success in a team-based environment, including leadership and employee development
**Demonstrated successful interaction with internal and external customers

> - As Transportation Manager for Ames' Midwest Region, in just over a year I cut hundreds of thousands of dollars from operating costs, improved productivity 12%, and contributed to the division's first profitable quarter ever.
>
> - For automotive-supplier Klein Auto Systems, I implemented a new loading system that improved efficiency more than 35% and enabled us to achieve same-day supply status for our top 10 accounts.
>
> I'm confident I can deliver similar results for your organization.
>
> In brief, I am an experienced transportation manager and project leader. I understand and apply state-of-the-art methodologies for continuous improvement of the distribution process; yet I realize that it is people who ultimately deliver results, and I am strongly focused on building relationships with employees, managers, suppliers, and customers as a primary tool for business success.

It's not essential that you compare your qualifications point by point with every requirement in a job description. Remember, your cover letter accompanies your resume, which provides much more detail. The main purpose of your cover letter is simply to create interest in talking with you to find out more. If you hit on your most important qualifications and most significant contributions—always in areas of interest to the people you are writing to—then you will pique their interest and motivate them to look at your resume and ultimately pick up the phone to contact you for an interview.

Of course, you will not always be referring to a job description when writing your cover letters. In those instances, do your best to determine what the employer's most pressing concerns are, and address those in your cover letter. If no position exists, refer to what you know about the company and the industry. Here is an example of the middle section of a cover letter that does just that:

> Today's manufacturing economy presents many challenges. To stay competitive, plants must constantly become more efficient. I believe that the best way to accomplish this is by involving all employees in the improvement initiatives. When production workers are invested and involved, they put their heart and soul into meeting (and often exceeding) goals.
>
> I put this philosophy into action as production supervisor at Western Widgets. To keep our costs competitive, we were challenged to increase efficiency by 10% without an investment in technology. I brainstormed with all of our production staff, and we broke down into teams to test three of their ideas. With a little

competition, everyone was motivated to make their idea work the best. As a result, we implemented two of the ideas on the production line, increased efficiency 12%, and rewarded every worker for his or her contribution.

If your cover letter can expand on a specific problem you've discussed in an initial phone call, so much the better. Here is an example:

In our discussion on Wednesday you mentioned the high level of absenteeism in the call center. I have some ideas and some experience that might help—for example, at Techline we were experiencing absenteeism as high as 20% that really hurt our response times. We set up a series of incentives that increased for every week, month, and quarter of perfect attendance. Employees knew they had control over their bonus payments and therefore took responsibility for their own attendance.

Not only that, we added team bonuses as well, so that team members encouraged their peers to come to work. As a result, our attendance improved to a steady 95%, we cut 30 seconds from our average response time, and the increased productivity more than covered the cost of the bonuses.

The theme that runs through all of these examples is results. Employers are interested in applicants who have performed well in their past positions, and sharing specific examples will help them understand how you can add value to their organization.

For your cover letters, you can expand on many of the results, examples, and success stories that are in your resume. However, it is never a good idea to transfer information word-for-word from your resume to your cover letter. Be sure that you say something different about the accomplishment, add more details, blend two or three accomplishments from your resume into one story for your cover letter, or otherwise change the information so that your cover letter is not a carbon copy of your resume.

Step 3: Close with an Action Statement

Thus far, your cover letter has opened on a strong note and then gone on to include relevant and compelling information in the middle section. Now you must keep the momentum going by closing with an assertive yet polite request to advance to the next step.

Close on a positive note and let the employer know you desire further contact. Better yet, tell the employer you will call to follow up, and be sure that you keep this promise.

In your closing, don't lose your focus on how you can help an employer solve problems. Rather than simply stating what you want, try to include information about what you can do for the employer. Here are a few examples:

> "Mr. Smith, I look forward to meeting with you on Monday (I'll be there at 10:00 sharp) and sharing my ideas for your Northeast distribution center."
>
> "I would appreciate the opportunity to meet with you and explore how my skills and experience can be of value to you. I will follow up with a phone call early next week and look forward to connecting with you in person."

Assertive vs. Aggressive

I recommend an assertive closing, but don't get too aggressive. Keep your closing polite, positive, and pleasant. It is always better to request than to demand. Consider the difference:

> **Assertive:** "I will call within the next few days to see if we can schedule a time to meet. I'd like to share my ideas for improving the productivity of your field technicians."
>
> **Aggressive:** "I will call you at 10:00 on Tuesday. Please be available to discuss my ideas for improving the productivity of your field technicians."
>
> **Assertive:** "I eagerly await your ideas and suggestions. I will call on Thursday in hopes of setting up a brief meeting at a time that is convenient for you."
>
> **Aggressive:** "Your support is important for my job search, and I eagerly await all the leads you can give me. I will call on Thursday to see what names you have collected thus far."

When Follow-up Isn't Possible

Sometimes you will be sending cover letters and resumes in response to "blind" ads and you won't know who is receiving your letter—or perhaps even what company it is going to. In those cases, your follow-up is limited—you cannot promise to call, for example. So how do you keep your closing assertive and action-oriented? Here are a few ideas:

"Because my qualifications appear to be an excellent fit for your needs, I look forward to the opportunity for an interview. You can reach me most easily on my cell phone (212-489-5612)."

"I look forward to learning more about this interesting opportunity and exploring the fit with my experience. I would be pleased to answer any quick questions you have by telephone (212-489-5612), and of course I'd like to meet with you at greater length in person. I am confident I can help your organization achieve its goals."

"May we schedule a time to talk soon? I am a strong candidate for this position and would like to share my ideas with you while learning more about your current and future challenges."

In most cases, your closing will be one paragraph long. Be brief, action-oriented, and focused on your ability to add value.

Disclosing Salary Information

It is quite likely that some of the ads you respond to will request or even demand salary information. What should you do?

My first recommendation is that you not share your salary history or salary requirements with employers at this stage. After all, you do not know much about the position. If it is a blind ad, you have not even been able to research the company or the industry. Why should you disclose information that can work against you, whether it is too high or too low?

Instead, I suggest that you choose one of these options:

- **Ignore it.** Research shows that employers will—almost 100 percent of the time—look at your resume anyway to see if you have the skills they are looking for.

- **Provide a range.** You might feel more comfortable responding to the request in some way. If so, I recommend that you first conduct salary research to learn average salaries for the position, then state your salary requirement in the form of a range. "I understand that typical salaries for this type of position are in the $45,000 to $55,000 range, and I anticipate a comparable salary from your company."

- **Respond if required.** Sometimes you will see an ad that states you "must" include salary information or your application will not be accepted. In these cases, I recommend that you reply with a range or a general rather than specific figure. "My annual compensation has been in the mid to high $70s for the last few years."

Be sure to keep copies of all of your cover letters so you'll know who you contacted, what you said, and what the next steps are.

On the following pages you will find a small selection of cover letters that apply all of the above guidelines and will give you further ideas for creating effective letters to accompany your resume.

Rafael Lewis

294 Aster Lane, Cincinnati, OH 45208
Home: (513) 739-1265 ● Mobile: (513) 230-0943 ● E-mail: raflewis@hotmail.com

April 30, 2008

Enquirer Box 719-A
Cincinnati, OH 45202

Re: CUSTOMER SERVICE MANAGER

Under my leadership, the customer service department of Tech-Line was transformed from a business liability to a competitive advantage for the company. We cut hold times by 75% and consistently performed at 95% of the world-class standard of 24-hour problem resolution.

As detailed in the enclosed resume, my background includes more than eight years of management experience complemented by a strong technical background in applications development. In all of my positions, I have developed solid collaborative relationships with business and technical departments of the company, and I have consistently demonstrated a customer-centric approach that is also sensitive to bottom-line priorities.

I can be a valuable addition to your team and look forward to a personal meeting to discuss how I can deliver results for your company.

Sincerely,

Rafael Lewis

enclosure

Figure 5.1: A cover letter for an experienced customer service manager.

Dear Ms. Gold:

My sister, Tracy Oswald, tells me that you are looking for a systems administrator for your growing San Francisco operation.

I am experienced, reliable, loyal, and customer-focused and would like to talk with you about joining your team.

The enclosed resume describes nearly 15 years of experience with Anthem Blue Cross/Blue Shield, during which I advanced to increasingly responsible technical positions. Whether working independently or with a team, I worked hard to provide the best possible service and support to my "customers." I was recognized for my strong technical skills, ability to guide less experienced support people, and 100% reliability.

A recent downsizing at Anthem caused my position to be eliminated, and I am looking for a new opportunity with a company like yours, where my technical abilities, positive attitude, and dedication will be valued.

I will call you next week in hopes of getting together soon.

Yours truly,

Kevin Oswald

****
My resume is attached as a Word document.

Figure 5.2: An e-mail cover letter for a systems administrator candidate.

TRICIA BILLINGS

London, England (through July 2008)
TriciaBillings@msn.com

April 30, 2008

Re: Market Development Manager: Posting #794-MDM

Your advertised opening for a Market Development Manager describes interesting challenges. My background and accomplishments seem to be a good match for your needs, and I'd like to explore this opportunity with you.

For 18 years I have delivered strong business results for company operations in Europe and the U.S. Most recently, I took on the challenge of rapidly growing Standard Tool's business in the U.K. In two years, we increased sales nearly four-fold through highly effective market-entry strategies, brand repositioning, and organizational restructuring.

Previously, with Global Supplies, I was instrumental in successful market entry into Western and Eastern Europe, with results that outperformed goals for both sales and profits.

May we schedule a time to talk? I am always accessible via e-mail and can arrange a phone call immediately or an in-person visit during one of my frequent trips to the U.S.

Thank you.

Sincerely,

Tricia Billings

enclosure: resume

Figure 5.3: A cover letter for a market development manager.

Jamie Van Horn

253 Silverton Trail, Phoenix, AZ 85017
602-779-1682 • jvanhorn@yahoo.com

April 30, 2008

Sally Osborne
Southwest District Manager
Pfizer Pharmaceuticals
6512 Scottsdale Boulevard
Phoenix, AZ 85010

Dear Ms. Osborne:

Sandra Lopez has suggested that I forward my resume to you for consideration for a current sales opening in the Southwest District of Pfizer Pharmaceuticals.

Through conversations and ride-alongs with Sandra, I have learned what it takes to be a successful pharmaceutical sales representative, and I am confident I have the drive, dedication, and proven skills that will enable me to quickly become productive. Highlights of my career experiences include:

- **Consistent performance above goals in direct-sales positions:**
  — **130%, 2007–2008**
  — **115%, 2006–2007**
  — **141%, 2005–2006**
- **Trend of sales growth in competitive environments:**
  — **25%, 15%, and 6% growth in diverse sales departments, 2003–2005**
  — **10% growth as a result of community marketing and visibility/ awareness campaigns, 2003–present**
- **25% year-over-year sales increase as sales manager**
- **Initiative and leadership in developing relationship-marketing programs**
- **Management experience and proven strengths in organization, planning, and follow-through**

I would like to meet with you to explore how my background and talents can benefit your company as a sales representative in the Greater Phoenix area, and I will call within a few days to get your thoughts and possibly schedule a meeting. Thank you.

Sincerely,

Figure 5.4: A cover letter for a pharmaceutical sales rep that demonstrates results.

Subject: Prep for our meeting on 5/5 re: Acct Exec position

Dear Ms. Anthony:

Thank you for the information you shared with regard to your Account Executive position. Your need to create quick growth for your new .Net publication is a great fit for my experience at Smythe Publications.

As Regional and National Sales Manager with Smythe, I have delivered results for every one of my multiple publications serving various audiences in the high-tech market:

- For our flagship publication, *C++ Calling,* I elevated sales 339% in a challenging market.
- Taking over two niche publications, I quickly generated new revenue from key target accounts including Sun and Dell.
- Handed a "dying" publication, I doubled ad sales in five months and grew the business so much that three new staff were added to handle the volume.
- For *Joe Java Journal,* in my first high-tech publishing assignment, I became the top salesperson and increased revenue 77% in six months.

In brief, I am a highly accomplished sales professional who gets results by listening to my customers and developing creative solutions that meet their needs. (I have the highest account retention rate at my company.) My background in selling diverse products and services gives me an exceptionally strong base in sales fundamentals, and I am driven to set and exceed aggressive goals.

I have been thinking about some ways to achieve a quick growth spurt in the emerging .Net marketplace, and I look forward to sharing these with you at our meeting at 10:30 on May 5. If you have any questions before then, you can always reach me at my mobile number, 415-292-1276.

Best regards,

Dale Gelman

****
Attached: Resume (MS Word .doc file)

Figure 5.5: An e-mail cover letter with a resume attachment.

Chris Angelos
152 Elm Street, Reading, MA 01867
(H) 781-942-0925 • (M) 781-204-9904 • angelos@verizon.net

April 30, 2008

Steven T. Edgerton
Executive Search Consultant
Biggs, Byers, Bailey & Bloggs
859 Madison Avenue, Suite 21B
New York, NY 10023

Dear Mr. Edgerton:

Thank you for spending some time on the phone with me today. Your firm's reputation as a leader in manufacturing-industry searches prompted my call, and I was glad to learn that you have several active searches that might fit my profile.

Building productivity, profitability, and efficiency in manufacturing operations is what I do best. For the past six years, I have led a custom-aluminum manufacturer to consistently high profitability while delivering strong results in all areas of operations:

- **100%** key customer satisfaction
- **100%** on-time delivery for our top account
- **100%** environmental regulatory compliance
- **99+%** quality
- **83%** reduction in production downtime
- **25%** reduction in inventory
- **15%, 20%,** and **25%** reductions in product, service, and utility costs
- **10%** sales growth with all major accounts

As a hands-on manager, I have practical working knowledge of every area of operations. I have instilled a "customer first" attitude top to bottom throughout the plant. My work ethic and reliability are exceptional (I haven't missed a scheduled day of work in 15 years), and I enjoy the challenge of continuously improving an already good operation.

The owner's decision to increase his own involvement and bring additional family members into the business is the reason for my current search. My record shows what I have done for the bottom line and our customers; I'm confident I can do the same as a Plant Manager or Production Supervisor for one of your clients.

I would like to schedule a meeting with you on my next trip to New York, and I will call you on Friday to find a convenient time.

Sincerely,

Chris Angelos

enclosure: resume

Figure 5.6: A follow-up letter sent after a phone interview.

Sharon Steiger

2490 Calumet Farm Drive, Cincinnati, OH 45249
513-204-7900 (mobile)
s_steiger@cinci.rr.com

April 30, 2008

Mr. Brandon Desmond
Chief Information Officer
Cincinnati Financial Services, Inc.
249 Vine Street
Cincinnati, OH 45202

Dear Mr. Desmond:

I am contacting you at the suggestion of Audra Pederson, who has told me about your expansion plans and need for experienced IT leadership.

Leading technology projects, teams, and organizations to support strategic business goals is what I do best. As Senior Technology Leader for Midwest Trust, I guided the massive technology conversion and integration projects that followed each of our 12 acquisitions—in each case, merging hundreds of financial products, systems, and services into our central technology systems, while providing a seamless transition to customers.

Just as importantly, my division supported business growth from $500 million to $6 billion with only a 25% increase in IT staff.

Of course, technology services are only as good as the technical staff that designs, implements, and supports them. I have found that there is no "trick" to keeping staff morale high and turnover low—rather, it relies on a top-down management attitude of respect, empowerment, continuous professional development, and teamwork. The proof of this approach can be seen in the 5% or lower turnover rate I maintained for over a decade.

I'd like to meet and discuss ways in which my leadership, technical, and managerial skills can be valuable to your organization. You may reach me at the above number; and I will try to reach you by phone in the next few days.

Sincerely,

Sharon Steiger

enclosure: resume

Figure 5.7: A cover letter that capitalizes on a networking contact.

Key Points: Chapter 5

- Send a cover letter with every resume.

- Immediately let your reader know why you are writing.

- Highlight your most notable accomplishments as a way to pique your reader's interest.

- Focus on your value and how you can solve problems for the employer, not on what *you* want.

- Recap key information from your resume without repeating items word-for-word.

- Use an assertive yet polite closing, and whenever possible take the initiative to follow up.

Chapter 6

Find a Job Fast

The best resume in the world does no good if it sits in a drawer or on a computer hard drive. No, you've got to put that resume out into the world, accompanied by a killer cover letter and a carefully planned strategy for finding the right opportunities.

This chapter provides a quick overview of the most effective job search activities. After all, it only makes sense to spend your time and energy on the efforts that will give you the best and the quickest results.

The single smartest strategy to pursue in looking for a new job is to pursue many different avenues. You never know where your next job is going to come from! You can find statistics about how *most* people find jobs, but that doesn't mean your transition is going to be like *most* people's. Also, there is no specific A-to-Z path you can follow to your next job. The more lines you have in the water, the better chance you have of catching a fish.

So let's examine five diverse avenues and how you can best use them to learn about job opportunities:

- Networking
- Internet job boards
- Newspaper ads (print and online)
- Executive recruiters
- Direct application to employers

Networking Is King!

Every survey of every population I've ever seen has shown that, by far, most people find their jobs through a personal connection—someone they know tells them about a job, or someone they know refers them to another contact who is the eventual source of a new job.

What this means to you is that you should get your network working for you.

Let's first define the term. Networking means, pure and simple, talking to people—telling them about your career plans, letting them know how they can help you, soliciting their advice, and asking for referrals to people at your target companies and in your target industries.

Notice I don't say "asking them for a job." Asking everyone you know for a job is the best way to turn off your network and make people uncomfortable about talking to you. Instead, rely on your friends, relatives, co-workers, and all of your personal and professional contacts to give you their advice, ideas, leads, and referrals. If they know of a job, don't worry—they'll tell you.

To capture the extraordinary job-finding abilities of your network, follow these simple rules:

- Be prepared. Before you initiate contact, prepare your message so that it is unambiguous, concise, and focused. Your contacts should come away with a clear understanding of what you're looking for, what you're good at, and the kinds of leads and referrals that will be of help to you.

- Offer to help your contacts. Networking is a two-way street, and if you go into it with a spirit of giving you are much more likely to get help in return.

- Accept all ideas, leads, and referrals—and follow up on them.

- Don't expect your network to find a job for you or do the work of your job search for you.

- Don't whine about unfair treatment, complain about what a hard time you're having, or say anything negative about your former boss or co-workers. While you're not expected to be upbeat all the time, remain professional and don't burden your network with your personal issues. (But do have a sounding board—a spouse, close friend, or professional counselor—to whom you can express all of the emotional upheaval that often accompanies a job transition.)

- Report back periodically to your network to let them know how you're doing, how helpful their ideas were, and what you need as your next step. This helps rejuvenate your network and keeps the good ideas flowing.

Internet Job Boards Are Jumping!

To many job seekers, the online job boards are a "black hole"—a bottomless pit into which they keep throwing resumes with no response. In truth, it can feel this way. Because it's so easy to apply for jobs, many people do, so the competition is fierce. And because automated scanners review those resumes for keywords, you must be a perfect match to rise to the top.

However, recent evidence suggests that results from the job boards are improving. In particular, entry- to mid-level professionals, technical people, and salespeople seem to get better-than-average results from this activity.

Because this option is viable, free, and easy, it certainly makes sense to use it. Just be cautious that you don't spend all your time throwing resumes into the void and praying for results. Follow these guidelines to maximize your success rate:

- Customize your resume. Although following the *30-Minute Resume Makeover* advice means your resume contains the vast majority of keywords for your target jobs, take the time to cross-check your content against the posting and adjust as necessary so you have a word-for-word keyword match—as accurate and appropriate to your background, of course.

- Include a cover letter. This may be "optional," but because it can give you a decided advantage, don't overlook this step. Stuff your cover letter with keywords, too.

- Create a quick, easy process to get your resumes out quickly. Don't worry about following up—just send it and forget it. If they're interested, they'll be in touch.

- Use some restraint—don't send out massive quantities of resumes for jobs for which you are only marginally qualified. It's a waste of your time and the company's time.

- Don't apply repeatedly to the same company (either different jobs or the same job); more is not better. If you are really interested in the company and your resume doesn't draw a response, look for other ways to get in contact. Your network is the first and best place to start.

- In addition to the major job boards (CareerBuilder.com, Indeed.com, Craigslist.org, Monster.com), don't overlook the many niche boards that serve your profession or your industry. You can find a great primer on online job searching at www.job-hunt.org, one of the Web's most informative career sites and a source for carefully vetted resources.

Newspapers Aren't Passé!

Traditional printed newspapers, business weeklies, and professional association publications can be an excellent source of job ads and job leads—particularly if you want to stay in your local area. Most major daily newspapers publish their careers section online as well as in print, so you have the option to look in either place—or in both. Sometimes it's easier to scan a dozen pages in the Sunday paper than it is to pump in keywords and sort through dozens or hundreds of irrelevant online listings to find the ones you want.

Here are several guidelines for the paper pursuit:

- Go through your publications with a highlighter and identify appropriate job openings, hiring trends, and other news related to your industry or your career.

- For blind ads, follow the advice given regarding job boards (see "Internet Job Boards Are Jumping!" in the preceding section). Customize your resume; include a cover letter; get your resume out quickly; send it and forget it.

- For ads that reveal the name of a local employer, before sending out a resume contact your network to see if you can get a referral to the hiring manager. If so, go directly to the source instead of or in addition to sending your resume to HR.

- Be alert to news about your target companies. You might learn something that will help you make a connection or make a great impression during the interview.

Recruiters Rock!

The most critical fact to remember with regard to recruiters is that they don't work for you—they work for the hiring company. So they are not "your" recruiter and won't try to "find a job for you."

But executive recruiters can be your very best friends during a job search—provided you have the precise set of skills, experience, and industry expertise their client (the employer) is looking for. Follow this advice to get the most from the recruiter relationship:

- Take the time to find out the recruiter's specialty areas before getting in touch. Otherwise, you'll create a poor impression, not to mention wasting the recruiter's time and your own. You can look through recruiter directories (check your local library) to find a list of appropriate recruiters, or simply phone the recruiters in your local area to ask about their specialty areas.

- When writing to recruiters, refer to "your client" or "your client's organization" rather than "your company."

- Send an e-mail cover letter with a resume attached, and call the next day to follow up. The purpose of this call should be to determine whether that recruiter is a good fit for you and to establish the basis for periodic contact. Be prepared to introduce yourself concisely with relevant information and some "wow" achievements.

- Don't expect to hear back from recruiters unless they have a job that's a potentially good fit for you.

- Understand the realities of recruitment. The recruiter has a mandate for the ideal candidate. If that recruiter doesn't think you are the right fit, there is nothing you can do to change his or her mind. Move on to the next opportunity!

- If you can help the recruiter by referring good candidates, do so. It's a win-win for all involved.

Direct Application Is Dandy!

Most employers of any size have dedicated career Web sites, where you can peruse jobs and submit your application directly to the company. Sometimes this process is easy and satisfying—you get immediate feedback and can always track the status of your application. Much more often, it is time-consuming, frustrating, and resembles the same "black hole" as the job boards. Still, it's certainly worth your while.

These guidelines will help you navigate the company career sites:

- Customize your resume. Take the time to cross-check your resume against the posting, then adjust your content as necessary.

- Include a cover letter mentioning why you want to work at that particular company.

- If you receive a confirmation number or other information related to your application, make note of it! If an individual's name is provided, be sure to write it down so you can follow up accordingly.

- Don't apply repeatedly to the same job, and don't apply to dozens of jobs at the same company.

- If you apply to more than one job, be sure your resume is customized for each—but make sure that comparing the two side by side won't reveal major differences or discrepancies.

Diversify Your Activities

As you create the plan for finding your next job, include all five of these avenues, and make sure your daily and weekly action plans include some efforts in each area.

Additional avenues you might pursue include—in decreasing order of effectiveness—career fairs, alumni associations and college career centers (for both current students and alumni of any age), temporary or permanent placement agencies, billboards or other public postings, and of course simply walking into a company and applying.

Whatever you choose to do, bear in mind—always—that looking for a job is hard work, and no one can do it but you. That's not to say you can't take advantage of professional services and automated tools to make things a bit easier and faster. But ultimately it is your responsibility and it must be you doing the bulk of the legwork, phone calls, e-mails, research, and evaluation of companies and opportunities. Beware of any person or company that promises to "find a job" for you or deliver access to the "hidden job market." For most of these services, the price is high and the customer satisfaction low.

But develop a diversified plan, pursue it vigorously, and you will end up with a great opportunity and a satisfying career. The experience and knowledge you gain during this transition will be valuable every time you make a move throughout your career. Keep your resume up to date with a periodic 30-Minute Resume Makeover, and you'll be ready for whatever comes your way!

Key Points: Chapter 6

- Use a diversified strategy for your job search, pursuing opportunities in many different channels.

- Spend the bulk of your time in networking activities because this is the proven "king" of all search strategies.

- Craft a careful message so that you give your network contacts everything they need to know to be able to help you.

- Create a fast and easy process to respond to job board and newspaper listings. Don't spend too much time on this activity, which typically yields poor results.

- To make recruiters an effective part of your search activities, understand how they work.

- Customize your resume when applying directly to companies on their career Web sites.

- Be wary of people or companies that promise to do the work for you; you must manage your own job search and ultimately your career.

Appendix

Resume Development Worksheet

In case you don't have even a basic resume to use as a starting point, here's a helpful worksheet. Use it to pull together all the information you'll need to start your resume and give it the 30-Minute Makeover.

RESUME DEVELOPMENT WORKSHEET

Header/Contact Information

Name: _____

Home address: _____

Home phone: _____

Cell phone: _____

E-mail address: _____

Headline ("who I am"): _____

Subheadings (major areas of expertise): _____

_____

Personal brand tagline: _____

_____

Summary paragraph: _____

_____

_____

_____

_____

(continued)

(continued)

_____

_____

_____

Keyword list: _____

_____

_____

_____

_____

"Wow" achievements (top 3–5 specific accomplishments of career)

_____

_____

_____

_____

_____

Professional Experience

Job #1 (most recent): _____

Company name, city, state: _____

Brief description of company: _____

Job title, dates of employment: _____

#1 achievement in this position: _____

_____

Brief summary of job duties: _____

_____

Specific accomplishments/highlights/contributions: _____

_____

_____

_____

_____

Job #2: _____

Company name, city, state: _____

Brief description of company: _____

Job title, dates of employment: _____

#1 achievement in this position: _____

_____

Brief summary of job duties: _____

_____

Specific accomplishments/highlights/contributions: _____

_____

_____

_____

Job #3: _____

Company name, city, state: _____

Brief description of company: _____

Job title, dates of employment: _____

#1 achievement in this position: _____

_____

Brief summary of job duties: _____

_____

Specific accomplishments/highlights/contributions: _____

_____

_____

(continued)

(continued)

_____

_____

Job #4 (most recent): _____

Company name, city, state: _____

Brief description of company: _____

Job title, dates of employment: _____

#1 achievement in this position: _____

_____

Brief summary of job duties: _____

_____

Specific accomplishments/highlights/contributions: _____

_____

_____

_____

_____

Job #5 (most recent): _____

Company name, city, state: _____

Brief description of company: _____

Job title, dates of employment: _____

#1 achievement in this position: _____

_____

Brief summary of job duties: _____

_____

Specific accomplishments/highlights/contributions: _____

_____

_____

_____

_____

Repeat as necessary for additional employment experience.

Education

Graduate Degree: _____

Year earned: _____

Major fields of study: _____

Name of school, city, state: _____

Academic honors: _____

_____

Undergraduate degree: _____

Year earned: _____

Major fields of study: _____

Academic honors: _____

Significant activities: _____

_____

International study: _____

_____

Additional Training / Certification: _____

_____

_____

(continued)

(continued)

Extras

Additional distinguishing information to include on resume.

_____

_____

_____

_____

_____

_____

_____

_____

_____

_____

Potential Red Flags

Notes regarding potential problem areas; be sure to address these before completing your resume.

_____

_____

_____

_____

_____

_____

_____

_____

_____

_____

Index

Notes

Notes